FOREIGN
AID
A · N · D
AMERICAN
PURPOSE

T.W. Schultz
Dec. 1988

FOREIGN
AID
A · N · D
AMERICAN
PURPOSE

Nicholas Eberstadt

With a foreword by Theodore W. Schultz

Nobel Laureate in Economic Science

American Enterprise Institute for Public Policy Research
Washington, D.C.

Distributed by arrangement with

National Book Network
4720 Boston Way   3 Henrietta Street
Lanham, MD 20706   London WC2E 8LU England

Library of Congress Cataloging-in-Publication Data
Eberstadt, Nick, 1955–
    Foreign aid and American purpose / Nicholas N.
Eberstadt.
        p.   cm. — (AEI studies ; 474)
    Includes bibliographies and index.
    ISBN 0-8447-3657-0.   ISBN 0-8447-3658-9 (pbk.)
    1. Economic assistance, American—History—20th
century.
    2. Technical assistance, American—History—20th
century.
    I. Title.   II. Series.
    HC60.E19   1988   88-15456
    338.91′73′01724—dc19   CIP

    ISBN 0-8447-3657-0 (alk. paper)
    ISBN 0-8447-3658-9 (pbk.: alk. paper)

    1 3 5 7 9 10 8 6 4 2

AEI Studies 474

Printed in the United States of America

For Mary

Contents

Acknowledgments

The essays in this volume have previously been published in the following places: chapter 1: *Commentary,* June 1985; chapter 2: *Commentary,* March 1985; chapter 3: *Wall Street Journal,* September 17, 1986; chapter 4: *National Interest,* Winter 1987/88; chapter 5: *This World,* Summer 1986, and, in slightly different form, Michael Novak, *Liberation Theology and the Liberal Society* (Washington, D.C.: American Enterprise Institute, 1987); chapter 6: Doug Bandow, ed., *U.S. Aid to the Developing World: A Free-Market Agenda* (Washington, D.C.: Heritage Foundation, 1985). All essays are reprinted with permission of the respective publishers; all rights are reserved.

Footnotes have been added to all essays in the interest of assisting readers who wish to pursue the issues and arguments in this collection in greater depth.

This volume has been published through a grant from the Sarah M. Scaife Foundation. I am happy to acknowledge its generous support for this project.

Foreword

Criticism of economic doctrines and society's institutions by economists is at a low ebb. Those who practice the art of forecasting are weak as critics. Economists who specialize in building elegant models appear to have a comparative advantage in academic competition. As the status of historical economics declines within economics, the short view suffices. What is forgotten is Jacob Viner's argument, "No matter how refined and how elaborate the analysis, it will still be . . . a structure on shifting sand."

The criticism that is lacking is fairly obvious. In my *Investing in People* I argued that there are few competent, critical studies of the particular economic doctrines of those United Nations organizations that are seriously debasing economics. Whereas the early economic doctrines of the church, as Viner has shown, were supported by considerable scholarship, the economic doctrines that prevail within the United Nations are not. It is to the lasting credit of Harry Johnson that he did challenge these doctrines: Peter Bauer's harsh dissents are another exception. National economic doctrines are abundant.

Nicholas Eberstadt has specialized in dissenting, protesting, and criticizing economic policies and doctrines. U.S. foreign aid, economic myths about Africa, and doctrines pertaining to economic development have long been on his agenda. His critical essays have become increasingly more telling. His early radical viewpoint moved him to do time in the Philippines, much of it at the International Rice Research Institute. During his year at the London School of Economics he struggled with the strong critical ideas of Peter Bauer. From his work for AID, the State Department, and the World Bank, he learned by doing.

Eberstadt's essays reach for the long view, during which the shifting sands of economic growth are important. His critical treatment of policy and doctrine is most timely in view of the low ebb of this part of economics.

THEODORE W. SCHULTZ
Charles L. Hutchinson
Distinguished Service Professor Emeritus,
University of Chicago

Introduction

Concern for the plight of distressed and needy populations in foreign lands is not new to American history—quite the contrary. Guided by a political creed that emphasized the universal and indivisible dignity of man, Americans throughout two centuries have been consistently attentive to the well-being of other populations.

This concern was evident even in the earliest and most dire days of the republic. The impulse to extend goodwill and assistance abroad was at first conspicuously constrained by the limits of the nation's power. Yet the government and the citizens who sustained it lent emergency aid resources to efforts that were understood to promote well-being beyond the boundaries of the republic itself. From the examples of the American Revolution and the U.S. Constitution and later through diplomatic activities that were to culminate in the Monroe Doctrine of 1823,[1] the United States encouraged the pursuit of independence and advanced the quest for liberty elsewhere in the Western Hemisphere. Later, private philanthropies and subscriptions raised funds to relieve stricken populations abroad; the Irish famine of the 1840s was but one of many foreign disasters that set such charitable efforts in motion.[2] Meanwhile, in China and

1

elsewhere, American missionaries and American-sponsored missions labored to extend the sway of Christianity, for it was in those days taken as obvious that the fate of a man's soul bore more than a passing relation to his ultimate well-being.

In the early years of the republic, American statesmen firmly believed the country's conduct might benefit even lands untouched by American power or largesse. It might do so, they hoped, through the force of the American example. In providing the world with proof that limited and lawful government could justly preside over consenting citizens, they saw the possibility that the American public's every action—domestic or international, momentous or mundane—might of itself be a boon to those who hungered for liberty in foreign lands.[3]

In the second half of the nineteenth century, the American example was itself severely tested—not by military threats from abroad but by moral challenges at home. After many decades of deferring the question, the nation was at last forced to confront the problem of slavery.[4] Shortly thereafter, the country faced a new choice about immigration: would the United States continue to welcome foreign settlers when they were, increasingly, impoverished refugees from regions where the American political tradition was unfamiliar? Ultimately, both U.S. ordeals were resolved with an unambiguous and consequential extension of citizenship to both old and new inhabitants.[5] At enormous cost, the American public had resoundingly reaffirmed the American example to the world. The nation demonstrated not only that it would live by the consequences of the truly revolutionary principles enunciated in its founding documents but that it would thrive by them.

With the arrival of the twentieth century, the

United States was a world power. Government and private citizens alike embraced ambitious undertakings without precedence in the American experience. A partial list of such enterprises would include the interlude of American trusteeship over Cuba, the Philippines, and other territories ceded by Madrid after defeat in the Spanish-American war; the incorporation by giants of industry of immense charities specifically charged with promoting "the well-being of mankind throughout the world";[6] and the colossal relief operations, organized and administered by Herbert Hoover, that saved millions of persons in war-ravaged Europe (and in Soviet Russia) from an all-but-certain death by starvation.[7] Yet if these efforts represented real innovations—as they did—they were nevertheless animated by the same universal principles that had guided earlier and more tentative expressions of American purpose abroad.

World War II was the beginning of a fateful departure from this pattern. As the European "concert of nations" bade its final farewell, the United States became the leading power in world affairs. By 1945, the country could decisively shape, if not actually dictate, the terms of the coming peace. For American statesmen, this was a chance to fashion a new world order—one that they hoped would serve the world better than the order that had so manifestly failed in the 1920s and 1930s. Well before the final Allied victory, American leaders were deeply involved with the details of the new order they intended to bring forth. Whatever their differences, these men were united in their belief that the new global order should be hospitable to America's political values; and in their conviction that this order could be underwritten only by American power.

In the postwar era, the application of American

power was to permit, and at times require, a new array of policies and organizations. One of the new postwar policies came to be known as "development assistance." That policy and its consequences are the focus of this book.

In the late 1940s, foreign aid was hardly a new entry in the annals of diplomacy. In classical Greece, for example, warring city-states had sometimes subsidized allied governments to advance the cause of victory against common enemies. Foreign aid as such was by no means unfamiliar to the United States, which had both benefited from it during its own revolution and argued in its earliest years the propriety of aid to revolutionary France. Nor was foreign aid unfamiliar to postwar America's electorate. Between 1940 and 1945 the country had effected the greatest wartime transfer of goods and material that the world has ever seen;* at today's prices, the net value of America's bequests to its military allies would far exceed $200 billion.[8]

Neither America nor any other country, however, had ever contemplated the sorts of aid policies that were formalized through President Truman's Point Four proposal in his 1949 State of the Union address. Unlike the Lend-Lease program and its predecessors, development assistance (or, as it was

---

*To this day, the United States maintains an aid program expressly for *security* assistance; military aid, however, accounts for a comparatively small portion of current American aid outlays, and is discussed only briefly in this book in chapters 2 and 6. (Calculated from William A. Brown, Jr., and Redvers Opie, *American Foreign Assistance* [Washington, D.C.: Brookings Institution, 1953], p. 82; and U.S. Bureau of the Census, *Statistical Abstract of the United States* [Washington, D.C.: Department of Commerce].)

originally termed, technical assistance) was to flow to countries at peace. Unlike reparations, these government-to-government payments were voluntary; unlike disaster relief, this new form of aid would not be occasioned by particular emergencies. It was instead to be a long-term and potentially worldwide program of continuing charitable disbursals, financed and administered through official channels.

The rationale for this assistance was also radically new. In theory, its chief criterion was to be material backwardness in recipient areas. Whatever its other intended benefits (and these were many), the proximate objective of technical assistance was the elevation of material living standards in foreign lands. This objective was clearly outlined, and indeed explicitly emphasized, at the very start of the program. As the president explained in his message to Congress on the Point Four proposals, his recommended legislation would "enable the United States, in cooperation with other countries, to assist the peoples of economically underdeveloped areas to raise their standards of living."[9] The same understanding was impressed upon the new institutions that had been created to lend stability to the postwar order. In September 1949, for example, the World Bank—which had at first devoted its resources to the reconstruction of a redevastated Europe—stated that its "basic mission [was] . . . to assist its member countries to raise production and living standards. . . . The Bank's basic objectives in this field are essentially the same as those of the Point Four program."[10]

Four decades have passed since this monumental effort at alleviating material poverty commenced. A vast transfer of potentially productive capital has indeed been executed. Adjusted for the intervening inflation, the net financial flow (both commercial and charitable) to aid-receiving countries from Western sources between the early 1950s and the mid-1980s would definitely exceed $1½ trillion and might actually amount to over $2 trillion.[11] By a variety of measures, material progress during these years appears to have been considerable in most of the countries that received development assistance or its earlier variants. Of themselves, however, these indications do not necessarily betoken the success of the policies in question, much less invite the satisfaction of the American populace that provided for them. Charity may always be relied upon to produce unintended results. The unintended consequences of development assistance have been both major and, in some important respects, adverse.

Over the past forty years, the arguments and debates about foreign aid have often been conducted on the plane of economic analysis—sometimes to the exclusion of all other considerations. The economic consequences of development assistance, and of other aid policies, are examined in the following chapters in some detail.

Economic reasoning alone, however, will not suffice in judging this new form of foreign policy. Our faculties for moral reasoning must be exercised as well. It is in this intangible, but very real, realm that American-initiated development assistance policies have been especially troubling.

Chapter 1, "The Perversion of Foreign Aid," traces the moral descent of these programs. From the standpoint of the principles embodied in them, the decline of America's aid policy has been so rapid as to suggest a sort of collapse. In scarcely twenty years, the emphasis on technical assistance and productive capacity has given way to a preoccupation with direct *budgetary* assistance: supporting social programs in foreign countries in the name of meeting basic human needs. Administrators who had once been instructed to condition the flow of aid on the policy climate in recipient countries are now instructed to focus their activities instead upon expanding the scope for official and concessional transfers. Careful review of specific projects has meanwhile proved to be increasingly inconvenient, conflicting as it does with the newly perceived need to transfer significant sums from Western taxpayers to third world treasuries.

In one sense, the devolution of postwar aid policy may be measured against the expectations of those who first framed it. In 1950, Secretary of State Dean G. Acheson assured a skeptical Congress that the president's $45 million Point Four request would set no ominous fiscal precedents. "By its very nature," he explained, "this is not and never will be a big money enterprise."[12] By the 1980s, the continuing "enterprise" was, evidently, substantially different from the program Acheson had endorsed, for it had become capable of absorbing enormous sums of money. In the first half of the 1980s, overseas development assistance from Western sources was being committed to governments of less-developed countries at a rate of about $40 billion a year.[13] Despite the intervening increase in per capita output in the less-developed countries, the allocation of development assistance to those countries was proceeding at over 200 times the level, in real terms, that had been envisioned in President Truman's initial technical assistance request.

The scale of outlays as such, however, is not the

7

heart of the problem. If need arose, after all, America could easily finance a much larger foreign aid program than the one it currently maintains. The larger problem is that, by the 1980s, American development assistance programs could not be said to forward or even in any systematic way to reflect the values and principles of the American political tradition. To some significant degree, in fact, official U.S. foreign aid policy had come to finance and promote practices that are inconsistent with the defense of liberty, inimical to the promotion of justice, and injurious to the nominal beneficiaries themselves—a point whose particulars are discussed in chapters 1, 3, and 4.

In retrospect, one may wonder whether the intellectual and moral decline that has beset official American efforts to finance development abroad was not in fact made likely by the very nature of the undertaking. However else it may at times have been described, development assistance was intended as an international antipoverty effort. Noble as the sentiments inspiring this project clearly were, the project itself may have been built on a precarious foundation. For poverty is a treacherous concept and an inconstant beacon by which to direct policy.

Practical and humane men have long appreciated this dilemma. Over 150 years ago, as Gertrude Himmelfarb has reminded us, the British *Poor Law Report* recognized and warned of "the mischievous ambiguity of the word *poor*."[14] As it indicated, many aspects of the human condition could be encompassed by the term. Indeed, by extending or restricting the usage of this elastic notion, poverty could be made to describe the starving or the comfortably fed; the industrious or the voluntarily idle; the destitute or those secure of livelihood; and populations whose prospects for material advance seem poor or those whose prospects seem all but ensured. "Poverty" is, in short, a consummately political word. In embracing a quest to alleviate international poverty, the United States appears unwittingly to have consigned itself to a form of political captivity, subordinating its policy to the particular meaning of poverty that might prevail at any particular moment in the international arena.

For the purposes of development assistance, poverty was defined in material terms—that is, with reference to the physical condition of recipient populations. While such a definition might sound straightforward, unobjectionable, and administratively prudent, it was in reality fraught with hazard. For in committing itself to a worldwide campaign against *physical* poverty, the United States had indicated that it was willing in principle to allow the condition of man to be separated from the nature and quality of his government.

Thus, wittingly or not, the U.S. government accepted as legitimate an approach to international affairs that was largely, and crudely, materialistic. Such an approach to development assistance has provided for a divorce between the ends and the means of American action—a divorce ultimately debasing for both. U.S. foreign policy may now attempt to purchase improvements in the physical circumstances of individual men and women even as it ignores the character and practices of the political authority under which these same men and women live. That is why, by 1988, some of the states that receive American development aid are openly contemptuous of the idea of liberty and of the principle of rule of law. In certain cases as will be detailed, they are indifferent even to the material well-being of their own subjects.

9

Vulnerable and politically voiceless populations abroad have suffered notably from the moral confusion that has corrupted development assistance policy. In the name of aiding the impoverished, our public charity has on more than one occasion empowered the very regimes principally responsible for local distress. Indeed, we must now ask ourselves whether our development aid did not at times make injurious practices and destructive policies feasible for governments that could not have sustained them without this source of external finance. This question is raised in various forms in chapters 2 ("Famine, Development, and Foreign Aid"), 3 ("'Human Capital' and Foreign Aid to Africa"), and 4 ("More Myths about Aid to Africa").

The moral tension newly embodied in American foreign policy through its aid programs has also impinged on the cause of freedom. For more than a generation, American officials have explained to domestic and international audiences that development assistance could foster, or perhaps even create, democracy abroad. It would do so, the argument goes, by hastening material progress, and with it the grounds for "stability." Although this argument may be well intentioned, it is also fundamentally flawed. After decades of public rhetoric equating the prospects for material advance with the prospects for democracy, it may be well to recall that prosperity is neither a necessary nor a sufficient condition for liberal democratic rule.

Our own history should tell us as much. When the Constitution was framed in 1787, life expectancy in the United States was almost certainly significantly lower than it is in sub-Saharan Africa today.[15] As late as the 1870s, moreover, per capita output in the

United States is estimated to have been substantially lower than the figures currently imputed to such places as Algeria, Jordan, and Mexico.[16] Conversely, high industrial output and near-universal literacy did not forestall the collapse of Weimar democracy or restrain the rise of Nazi totalitarianism in Germany. More recently, we have the example of Cuba—a nation that enjoyed one of the highest standards of living among Latin American states until Fidel Castro came to power; it has since become one of the poorest in the hemisphere, as well as the most unfree. The list might go on, but the implications are clear: material prosperity might be desirable for a variety of reasons, but it is neither a prerequisite for free and democratic rule nor a guarantee against those forces that might undermine such rule from within.

Indeed, the notion that lawful democratic rule should be dependent upon the prospects for material blandishments, much less blandishments from foreign lands, is not only inconsistent with the concepts of liberty and self-government but subversive of them. We see as much in Latin America today, where debtor governments are demanding that their loans from foreign creditors be converted ex post facto into charitable grants, lest repayment endanger democratic tendencies throughout the region. As I argue in chapter 5 ("Democracy and the 'Debt Crisis' in Latin America: A Comment"), what imperils the democratic prospects for Latin America today is not so much the debt itself (which in most cases could be redeemed by the sale of government assets) as the explicit unwillingness of various governments to honor their contracted obligations.[17] Over the years, the United States has extended considerable sums of public charity to the governments of Latin America. One might well wonder how these transfers have affected the attitudes toward accountability and rule of law that Latin American leaders are inadvertently revealing today as they attempt to renege on their international obligations.

But perhaps the most important unintended consequence of the new foreign aid policies has been their impact on the perception of the American example elsewhere in the world. In elevating the material transformation of living standards to an objective that should guide American policy, the United States has necessarily diminished the standing of certain other principles. The principle of liberty, for example, cannot easily coexist with the various intrusions into the private sphere that development planning has in various lands demanded. Nor is the proclaimed universal dignity of man reinforced by evidence that the American state will propose and even finance for other peoples policies that would be unthinkable—indeed, unconstitutional—at home.

If American foreign aid policies are to reaffirm our national principles, they will require sustained and unflinching reexamination. Chapter 6 ("Recommendations for Restoring Purpose to American Foreign Aid in the 1980s") provides one view of some ways in which the moral philosophy and practical effectiveness of U.S. foreign aid policy might be improved. These suggestions are not exhaustive, nor are they meant to preclude alternative suggestions for restoring purpose to this area of our foreign policy.

The purposes of American foreign aid and American foreign policy should be one. American power shall always be required to preserve and protect the United States, so that the most promising experiment in limited and constitutional self-government the world has yet known may continue its efforts at self-perfection. But so long as the example of the American republic is lost on foreign lands, the experiment will be forever incomplete. As the late Eric Hoffer once wrote, "There is an America hidden in the soil of every country and in the soul of every people. It is our task to help common people everywhere discover their America at home."[18]

If the United States is true to the beliefs and principles in which its power is constituted, its international conduct will of itself aid the vulnerable, the distressed, the voiceless, and the endangered in foreign lands in a way that monetary computations alone will never be adequate to measure.

Notes

1. William R. Manning, ed., *Diplomatic Correspondence of the United States Concerning the Independence of the Latin American Nations,* vol. I (New York: Oxford University Press, 1924), pp. 6–218.

2. Merle Curti, *American Philanthropy Abroad: A History* (New Brunswick, N.J.: Rutgers University Press, 1963), pp. 41–64.

3. Consider, for example, the words of Washington's Farewell Address:

> It will be worthy of a free, enlightened, and at no distant period a great nation to give to mankind the magnanimous and too novel example of a people always guided by an exalted justice and benevolence.

4. For a thoughtful discussion of this problem, see Herbert J. Storing, "Slavery and the Moral Foundations of the American Republic," in Robert A. Horowitz, ed., *The Moral Foundations of the American Republic* (Charlottesville, Va.: University of Virginia Press, 1986), pp. 313–32.

5. One measure of this extension may be had in the election process. In 1860, about 4.7 million ballots were cast in the presidential election. In 1896, the corresponding figure was 13.9 million—almost a tripling in a mere thirty-six years. U.S. Bureau of

the Census, *Historical Statistics of the United States: Colonial Times through 1970*, part II (Washington, D.C.: Department of Commerce), pp. 1079, 1080.

6. To quote from the seal of the Rockefeller Foundation.

7. One of the more interesting accounts of this venture is Hoover's own. See Herbert C. Hoover, *The Memoirs of Herbert Hoover: Years Of Adventure 1874–1920*. (New York: Macmillan Co., 1952), pp. 132–430.

8. Calculated from William A. Brown, Jr., and Redvers Opie, *American Foreign Assistance* (Washington, D.C.: Brookings Institution, 1953), p. 82; and U.S. Bureau of the Census, *Statistical Abstract of the United States* (Washington, D.C.: Department of Commerce), various issues.

9. Reprinted in the U.S. Department of State, *Bulletin*, July 12, 1949, p. 184.

10. International Bank for Reconstruction and Development, *Fourth Annual Report to the Board Of Governors, 1948–1949* (Washington, D.C.: IBRD, 1949), pp. 5, 7.

11. See chapter 2 in this book.

12. Dean G. Acheson, "Point Four Legislation," in Acheson, *Strengthening the Forces of Freedom: Selected Speeches and Statements of Secretary of State Acheson, February 1949–April 1950* (Washington, D.C.: Department of State, 1950), p. 71.

13. Organization for Economic Cooperation and Development, *Geographical Distribution of Financial Flows: Disbursements, Commitments, Economic Indicators 1982/1985* (Paris: OECD, 1987), p. 33.

14. *Report from His Majesty's Commissioners for Inquiring into the Administration and Practical Operation of the Poor Laws* (London, 1834), p. 156, quoted in Gertrude Himmelfarb, *The Idea of Poverty: England in the Early Industrial Age* (New York: Vintage Books, 1985), p. 523.

15. The United Nations Department of International Economic and Social Affairs places a figure of forty-nine on the life expectation at birth for those born on the continent of Africa, excluding northern Africa, for the period 1980–1985. By contrast, life expectancy at birth in the state of Massachusetts for the white population only was under forty in 1850. One may expect that life expectancy for the entire U.S. population would have been even lower in 1850, and lower still in earlier decades. Figures derived from Department of International Economic and

INTRODUCTION

Social Affairs, *Demographic Indicators of Countries: Estimates and Projections as Assessed in 1980* (New York: United Nations, 1982); and *Historical Statistics of the United States: Colonial Times through 1970,* part I (Washington, D.C.: Bureau of the Census, 1975), p. 56.

16. The U.S. Bureau of the Census produced an estimate for per capita U.S. gross national product (GNP) for 1869–1978; deflated against the producer price index, this would be about $1,360 in 1984 dollars. By contrast, the World Bank figures for 1984 GNP per capita are $1,570 for Jordan, $2,040 for Mexico, and $2,410 for Algeria. Derived from *Historical Statistics of the United States,* p. 224; *Statistical Abstract of the United States 1987,* p. 454; and World Bank, *World Development Report 1986* (New York: Oxford University Press, 1986), p. 181.

17. One may recall that the United States itself suffered a severe debt burden in its earliest years. By 1792 this debt, accumulated largely during the Revolutionary War and the short-lived state framed by the Articles of Confederation, amounted to $77 million—over four times the country's annual export earnings, and more than twenty times its total tax revenue. By many of the measures currently used to assess debt burden, the U.S. position would appear to have been more serious than those of many states that declared their inability to honor their financial obligations in the 1980s. There were voices in the United States asserting that the American experiment would be imperiled if the new republic assumed these debts (a substantial portion of which had been contracted to persons and governments overseas). A variety of excuses and rationales for reneging upon these debts were also proposed. In the end, however, the debts were assumed and honored. Alexander Hamilton, first secretary of the Treasury, expressed the sentiment that carried the day. "Establish that a government may decline a provision for its debts, though able to make it," he wrote, "and you overthrow all public morality, you unhinge all principles that must preserve the limits of free constitutions—you have anarchy, despotism, or what you please, but you have no *just* or *regular* government." (Figures derived from *Historical Statistics of the United States,* and *World Development Report 1986;* Hamilton quotation from Morton J. Frisch, ed., *Selected Writings and Speeches of Alexander Hamilton* (Washington, D.C.: American Enterprise Institute, 1985), p. 416.

15

18. Eric Hoffer, *First Things, Last Things* (New York: Harper & Row, 1974), p. 85. I am indebted to Herbert E. Meyer for this reference.

ONE

The Perversion of Foreign Aid

The attitude of the American people toward the world's poor, and toward our government's effort to attend to their distress, is seldom examined by those who frame our policies toward the international economy and the less-developed regions of the earth. It is instructive, however, to listen to what the American people have to say.

Surveys of public opinion consistently show a deep concern about the plight of needy people in other countries—a concern higher among the public at large than among those groups pollsters designate as "public-opinion leaders." While attitudes about most other aspects of foreign policy tend to vary with the times, the public's interest in aiding the desperately poor has remained remarkably constant. In 1982, as in previous years, nearly 60 percent of the respondents polled by the Chicago Council on Foreign Relations said they viewed "combating world hunger" as a "very important" objective for the United States; only 5 percent felt it to be "not important." As in previous surveys, combating world hunger ranked far ahead of "protecting American business abroad," and even ahead of "defending our allies' security" or "matching Soviet military strength," as an international concern.[1] Although these results may surprise some who consider themselves experts on foreign policy, they are not a fluke; to the contrary, they are in keeping with a wide range of findings from other polls.

Paradoxically, while the public's commitment to aiding the wretched of the earth gives all the signs of an unwavering consensus, its attitude toward foreign aid *programs* appears to be thoroughly hostile. Since 1974 the Chicago Council on Foreign Relations has asked respondents to volunteer their views of "the 2 or 3 biggest foreign policy problems facing the nation today." "Reducing foreign aid" is always one of the two top concerns. In these surveys neither the arms race, nor the threat of nuclear war, nor even relations with the Soviet Union has yet evoked the sort of response elicited by the idea of cutting foreign aid, which is by far the most unpopular program in the federal budget. In 1978—foreign aid's "best" year in the Chicago Council surveys—over four times as many interviewees favored cutbacks as approved of increases, leaving the program with a net rating of minus 39 percent. Even at the height of the disillusionment with the Vietnam war or on the eve of the "Reagan revolution," neither defense nor domestic welfare was held in such low esteem.

What can explain these strong—and yet apparently contradictory—feelings about helping the world's poor? One possibility is that they are only a specific example of a more general proposition: that the public's opinions about international problems are ill-considered, volatile, and vaguely irrational. But there is also a perfectly logical explanation for this

18

ostensible paradox. The American public may think its government's programs for aiding the world's poor defective or positively injurious. On this view, the stronger the public's commitment to the world's poor, the more forcefully it would reject programs that seem untrue to that commitment.

Interestingly enough, America's elites do not appear to share the deep misgivings of the public about U.S. foreign aid programs. According to a number of surveys, the overseas relief, development, and security policies that our people find so objectionable are considered utterly unexceptionable by our "public opinion leaders." Such surveys typically indicate that leaders view foreign aid as a nonissue.

This cleavage between the public and the opinion makers is highly significant. At different times in American history the general public has come to an understanding about the world before its leaders. We are now at such a point. The American people seem to recognize an important fact about world affairs that continues to elude their leaders—namely, that the American government's efforts to bring relief, prosperity, and security to impoverished peoples in other countries have gone seriously wrong.

The Beginnings of U.S. Foreign Aid

The descent of our foreign aid policies from their original purposes is a poignant story. Its outlines must be recounted, if only to recall how far we have strayed from our initial objectives and principles.

America's policies toward the international economy and the "backward areas" (as the "South" was then called) were fashioned, in the early days after World War II, by idealists whose vision had been tempered by hard times. America had suffered through more than a decade of economic depression and had then spent four years embroiled in a war of total mobilization against antidemocratic regimes that had gained control over several of the world's major industrial societies. America's leaders were determined that such events not be repeated.

Their ideas for rebuilding the world economy were shaped not only by their understanding of the causes behind the Depression, but by their memory and understanding of the international economic order that had existed before World War I.

As they knew, and as economic historians have since confirmed, the late nineteenth–early twentieth century was an era of widespread economic growth— not only in sovereign or imperial nations, but in many colonies as well. This growth had been made possible by technical advances, but it was propelled by a dramatic increase in trade and international flows of private capital, which served as conduits for the transfer of information, productive knowledge, and skills.

Although the architects of the postwar order wished to rebuild this framework, there was to be a crucial difference. Before World War I a system of empires and colonies had provided the political underpinnings for the financial and monetary arrangements of the world. America's leaders, however, were anti-imperialist; before World War II and after it, they were proponents of decolonization and national self-determination. Thus, toward the end of the second war, American statesmen began to create a "liberal international order" in which it would be possible to have, in effect, both bread and freedom: to capture the most beneficial economic workings of the trade and finance arrangements associated with the Age of

Imperialism and at the same time to protect the weaker peoples of the world against imperial subjugation and antidemocratic oppression.

The instruments devised to meet these objectives were, respectively, the Bretton Woods institutions—the International Monetary Fund (IMF) and the International Bank for Reconstruction and Development (the World Bank)—and the United Nations. In laying a base for international material progress, perhaps the more important of the economic agencies was the IMF. In theory, it provided a mechanism for the international convertibility of all members' currencies; in practice, it established the American dollar as the world currency, the new medium of international trade. This guarantee removed an enormous risk in international trade, one which had proved so dangerous between the wars for rich and poor regions alike.

Investment as well as trade had been a vehicle of international progress in the earlier era. The World Bank was to attend to some of the risks of putting private capital to work in poor or devastated areas. The bank's Articles of Agreement outlined its mission succinctly: "to facilitate investment for productive purposes . . . to promote private foreign investment by means of guarantees . . . and when private capital [is] not available on reasonable terms, to supplement private investment."[2] The U.S. Treasury Department, which would underwrite much of the World Bank's operations, had a similar understanding of its purposes. In the words of one analyst: "The Bank would encourage private investors to undertake international lending by guaranteeing international loans *through the usual investment channels* and by participating with private investors in such loans. *In exceptional cases,* where private capital is not available, the Bank would make loans out of its own resources" (emphasis added).[3]

The key to improving a nation's access to international capital, the early statements of the bank explained, was its "investment climate." This phrase is no longer in common usage, but its meaning remains fairly clear. It referred, if obliquely, to the economic and social policies promoted by the state—including its tax policies, its budget policies, its monetary and credit policies, its foreign exchange policies, its trade policies, its public investment policies, its legal system, and the extent to which formal and informal restrictions were placed upon people engaging in economic activity. The World Bank was, in these early days, extremely serious about the question of "investment climate." It went so far as to sanction a practice known as "strategic non-lending"[4]—abstaining from participation in loans to certain nations, even if they appeared creditworthy in the technical sense, because their economic policies were leading them, and the world community, in the wrong direction.

Recovery after World War II

What was the right direction? In his last address to Congress, President Roosevelt warned that "we cannot succeed in building a peaceful world unless we build an economically healthy world."[5] "Economic health," in Roosevelt's vision, depended upon both the international environment *and* the actions of individual countries. Even in regions of severe wartime devastation or acute mass poverty, recovery and growth were to be stimulated primarily by domestic effort. Roosevelt was firm on this point:

22

The main job of restoration is not one of relief. It is one of reconstruction which must be largely done by local people and their governments. They will provide the labor, the local money, and most of the materials. The same is true for all of the many plans for the improvement of transportation, agriculture, industry, and housing that are essential to the development of the economically backward areas of the world.[6]

Roosevelt and the men around him were not hostile to the idea of foreign aid. They had, after all, devised the Lend-Lease program, by far the greatest foreign aid program the world had ever seen (over $200 billion by today's prices). It was their unshakable conviction, however, that foreign aid should meet exacting standards. Its purposes were expected to be clear and morally legitimate; the programs that it fashioned should prosecute these objectives directly and effectively.

American relief efforts during and immediately after World War II were conditioned by this understanding and proved eminently successful. Protracted war had destroyed the local economic base throughout Europe and Asia. In many areas, mass starvation seemed a real possibility; in the months after defeat, for example, Germany's infant mortality rate was higher than Sahelian Africa's is thought to be today. To prevent a widespread loss of life, the United States had prevailed upon the United Nations to organize a Relief and Rehabilitation Agency (UNRRA). UNRRA was charged with providing "only those immediate relief needs which cannot be met out of the resources of the countries involved." Since it was understood that the danger of postwar famines was a temporary problem and would resolve itself as civil order and economic activity resumed in stricken regions, UNRRA's mandate was explicitly limited. UNRRA made clear its intentions to pull out after the first adequate harvest in an afflicted country—and kept its word. By 1947 the threat of mass famine in non-Communist nations had been averted; for the first (and possibly last) time in the UN's history, an agency was disbanded after successfully meeting the problem it was created to solve.

The next great application of American public resources in foreign lands, the Marshall Plan, was likewise considered a resounding success. The "European Recovery Act" brought together a variety of heretofore disparate American concerns. In contributing to the restoration of the Western European economies, it created a natural bulwark against the imperialistic ambitions of our erstwhile allies, the Soviets; it strengthened the foundations of the postwar economic order, which would require larger markets and greater supplies of private capital than America itself could offer if the rest of the world was to be drawn rapidly out of poverty; and it satisfied the American urge to assist endangered peoples overseas who shared our ideals and values.

In retrospect it can be seen that the accomplishments attributed to the Marshall Plan—a venture originally undertaken as a gamble—may have inspired a certain confusion about the potentialities of foreign aid under less extraordinary circumstances. Its unique marriage of strategic, economic, and humanitarian objectives would later give rise to the notion that foreign aid *naturally* wedded these distinct, and often contradictory, concerns.

In addition, the rapid Western European recovery was to mislead proponents of aid about the pace of progress that might be expected in under-developed areas, since it was widely forgotten that Western Europe was *restoring* itself to prewar levels of production activity. And with the restoration of Western Europe's economic health, the actual role of specific Marshall Plan policies in advancing or retarding recovery and economic progress was quickly submerged. Today only a handful of economic historians seem to remember that some of the policies advocated by Marshall Plan administrators, and tied to Marshall Plan aid, seemed to lead to inflation, a diminution of local savings, and economic stagnation—or that West Germany's economic boom did not begin until after Konrad Adenauer and his finance minister, Ludwig Erhard, had repudiated and reversed the policies that Marshall Plan aid was financing in other Western European nations.[7]

Development Assistance in the 1950s

Development assistance to low-income countries began in 1949, on the heels of the Marshall Plan. It was a new and radical idea in international relations. Unlike emergency relief, it was not framed in response to disaster. Unlike reparations, it was a state-to-state resource transfer prompted by volition, not indemnity. Unlike military aid or security assistance, it was not meant, in any immediate sense, to apply American will to distant regions of the earth.

Development assistance, as outlined in President Truman's Point Four program in his 1949 State of the Union address, reflected the American preference that other peoples avail themselves of the good things the twentieth century had to offer, including the skills and knowledge that made mass affluence possible. It was consistent with our vision of the postwar world. The United States had already created an international monetary and financial system that could contribute to a nation's economic advancement. We were now stating our willingness to help interested governments move their countries into the international economic updraft that the new order had made possible.

The idea of such assistance—of fostering the competence of new governments to deal with their nations' economic problems—received an enthusiastic reception from the world community. By the end of 1949 the United Nations had unanimously endorsed an international plan of action modeled directly on America's Point Four programs, though more modest in resources and scope.

The leitmotif of development assistance in its first few years was the connection between the policies and actions of governments in poor nations and their economic consequences. This connection was taken to be inescapable and obvious. Alluding to the "shortage" of Western capital in the less-developed countries—a problem that agitated many leaders in Latin America, Asia, and Africa at the time—Truman's assistant secretary of state for economic affairs observed that "the real decision must be made by these countries themselves, since only they can decide whether they want our capital to participate in their development. If they want it, they must, in turn, create the 'climate' to attract it."[8]

Nor was this perspective a matter of partisan dispute. Early in 1953, President Eisenhower's assistant secretary of state for economic affairs warned Congress that the limits on the effectiveness of our technical assistance programs came from the attitude of recipient governments: "There is a strong tendency to build steel mills when the best economic interest of that particular country would be served by growing a little more food. . . . But the attraction of being self-sufficient, of having these monuments of industry . . . seems to be so great that we have difficulties in getting them to understand wherein their own economic salvation lies."9

Development assistance as America envisioned it, unfortunately, was not quite what the new, nationalist elites in less-developed countries were looking for. Regardless of their professed political ideologies, these new regimes were almost uniformly preoccupied with augmenting the power of the state apparatus under their control. To many stewards of new states in the 1950s, the goal of building state power seemed, indeed, to be threatened by the liberal international economic order the United States was promoting. An orientation toward international markets and free flows of foreign capital might remove vital decisions about national destiny from their hands. What seemed more in keeping with their desire to focus the national will through the medium of government was some system of central economic planning.

This approach to nation building, later dignified by the title development planning, was in fact an application and perfection of the techniques the combatant powers had used to marshal and apply resources against one another in World War II. Around the globe, poor societies in the 1950s were, in effect, putting themselves on a wartime footing. They were going long on steel and short on food, relying on trade where they must, but on autarky where they might.

The extent to which this emphasis on command

27

planning clashed with the American conception of the function of development assistance was not immediately appreciated in the United States—where, after all, the popular preoccupation was with demilitarizing the economy as quickly as possible and with disassembling wartime economic controls so that the tempo of civilian life might resume. If this conflict in time helped bring about a very large shift in American ideas, in the early 1950s such changes were still far off. The United States had not only firm principles but also clear operational rules by which to guide its foreign aid policies. It attempted to separate overseas humanitarian aid from the economic interests of lobby groups at home. It made scrupulous distinctions between grants (which were charitable) and loans (which were to be commercial). Perhaps most important, it let it be known that there was a difference between military aid and development assistance and that the demarcation was essential to the purposes and prospects of both programs.

Departures from First Principles

One by one, these precepts about foreign aid were to fall.

The first abrupt departure occurred in 1954, when Congress authorized the Food for Peace program. On the East Coast, Food for Peace was justified as a humanitarian gesture by which American bounty could be put to the service of a hungry world; in the Midwest its workings were perhaps more honestly discussed. The champion of Food for Peace, Senator Hubert Humphrey, represented Minnesota, a state then beset by agricultural "overproduction." So long as the farmers' ability to produce outstripped the

market's demand for their produce, competitive re-
structuring of the farming industry would be inevitable, and, just as inevitably, it would be small farmers
who would be "restructured" off the land. These were
Senator Humphrey's constituents, and the Food for
Peace program, P.L. 480, addressed their problems.
P.L. 480 would authorize the purchase of massive
quantities of grain and other foodstuffs, subsidizing
their sale in the markets of poor countries or giving
food outright to governments.

For American farmers, the immediate impact of
P.L. 480 legislation was incontestably beneficial. For
the poor countries, the consequences were more am-
biguous. Heavily subsidized American imports very
often drove down local food prices; while this might
not have raised qualms in capitals intent upon forced-
pace industrialization, it nevertheless caused problems in rural hinterlands, where standards of living
were, typically, significantly lower than in the cities.

What is more, recipient governments often re-
sold the food America gave them for cash, so that they
could pursue projects that foreign lenders had denied them as economically unwise. A concessionary
device permitting recipient governments to repay
"food loans" in their own local currencies relieved
them of the pressure to value their foreign exchange
realistically, with predictable consequences for both
budget discipline and export incentives. (This also
paved the way for several international economic
panics, as when the Indian government suddenly dis-
covered it owed the United States more rupees than it
had in central reserves—and nationalized the entire
private banking system to compensate.)

Perhaps most tellingly, only a tiny fraction of P.L.
480's allocations was earmarked for regions hit by

famine or disaster. This fact was not lost on overseas observers, who had been warned by Marxists and other anti-Americans that the United States would export its own domestic economic problems and call the result charity.

The next radical deviation from principle came over the issue of "soft," or subsidized, loans. In 1946, American authorities had resolved that concessionary loans to foreign governments would have no place among the techniques of American statecraft; such loans, it was felt, would create a dangerous and needless confusion between charity and commerce. After our first soft loan, a large one to the United Kingdom to stabilize the sterling-based currencies, our National Advisory Council on Monetary and Financial Problems, which had sanctioned the offering, stated: "It is the view of the Council that the British case is unique, and will not be a precedent for loans to any other country."[10]

Within ten years, soft loans were becoming a preferred vehicle for U.S. foreign aid. Soft loans seemed to vitiate the need for hard choices. Skeptical inquiries from taxpayers over specific projects could be deflected by assurances that the United States expected in time to be fully repaid on its principal. Foreign governments would hear that soft loans gave them great financial leverage, since along with the concessionary bequest the arrangement provided a large pool of working capital. Soft loans thus seemed to offer protection to those aid initiatives whose usefulness was most open to question: yet this naturally made the loans a magnet for precisely those proposals that were least justifiable and most likely to waste resources. If soft loans at this time seemed like a cheap way of paying for foreign aid, it was only because one of their major costs had been forgotten: their impact on beneficiary governments' conception of, and attitude toward, capital transfer from abroad.

In 1948 the president of the World Bank had urged member nations not to fall into the trap of soft lending;[11] by 1959, the idea of a soft-loan facility *at the bank* was gaining acceptance; by 1961, this facility, the International Development Association (IDA), was established under World Bank auspices and with American blessings. Two decades earlier, a principal American proponent of a world bank, Secretary of the Treasury Henry Morgenthau, had said that the institution he was proposing would "scrupulously avoid undertaking loans that private investors are willing to make on reasonable terms."[12] IDA was true to the late secretary's wish only in the sense that the sorts of projects it encouraged, and the terms that it financed, were generally unlikely to be attractive to private investors.

Military and Development Assistance

The most fateful departure from previously enunciated principles of foreign aid, however, concerned the separation of military and development assistance. The Eisenhower years saw a profound shift in American foreign aid patterns. Between 1949 and 1953, military grants and political aid for beleaguered but friendly regimes had accounted for scarcely a sixth of our foreign aid; between 1953 and 1961 they made up over half our bequests.

Security assistance was a calculated response to a pressing problem. Shortly after the victory of the Communist armies on the Chinese mainland, Communist forces from North Korea attacked our allies in

31

the south and drew us into war. Strengthening the defensive capability of the states in our alliance system seemed the surest way to deter further outside attacks. There was also a widespread threat, in relatively open societies, of internal subversion by armed, and generally antidemocratic, domestic groups. Security assistance was to address this problem as well: it included not only military aid but police training, political advice, covert activities, and unrestricted financial bequests just to buy time (and thereby, with luck, political stability).

Military-security assistance proved to be a highly effective program. With American aid, South Korea and Taiwan were able to secure themselves against potential enemies. Greece and Turkey were stabilized and strengthened, both militarily and politically. Insurgencies were suppressed in, among other places, the Philippines and Thailand. In Iran, a demagogue who was deemed anti-American was turned out of office, and the shah (whom we took to be pro-American) was returned to the throne from which he had been deposed. There were many other, less heralded, achievements as well.

In the late 1950s and early 1960s, security assistance had widespread public support, while development aid was not nearly so well regarded. Hence, to win acceptance for their overall foreign aid programs, American statesmen began to draw on the legitimacy of security assistance to protect, and even conceal, development aid.

The process began with a change in legislation: the 1953 Mutual Security Act, which for the purposes of congressional appropriations linked development aid to security assistance. Even so, the two programs were kept operationally—and conceptually—distinct.

Eric Johnston, at the time Eisenhower's Point Four adviser, spoke for the administration when he said, "I think the Point Four program . . . should not in any way be confused with military aid to countries."[13]

That distinction was lost during the Kennedy administration. President Kennedy went so far as to argue that development aid *was* security assistance and therefore that advocates of a strong American security posture should support development bequests. As he put it: "I urge those who want to do something for the United States, for this cause, to channel their energies behind the new foreign-aid program to help prevent the social injustice and economic chaos upon which subversion and revolt feeds."[14] The "new foreign-aid program" to which he referred was the Agency for International Development (USAID), the organization that supervises and administers America's development programs in less-developed countries to this very day.

In attempting to broaden and strengthen the domestic constituency behind development spending, President Kennedy had, perhaps accidentally, fundamentally altered the understanding of what development assistance was supposed to be. No longer was it a transfer of skills and a building of basic infrastructure so that governments of poor societies might better take advantage of the economic opportunities afforded them by growing international markets. It was now a program to quell domestic discontent in low-income regions—linking aid to stability through a series of complex syllogisms, which ultimately equated rising living standards with diminishing political opposition. This attitude, at once cynical and naive, suggested that counterinsurgency and the diffusion of agricultural research were part and parcel of a single process, differing only in degree. Given this view of the world, Vietnam was in one sense an accident only waiting to happen.

The Gutting of AID

Even twenty years after the start of rapid escalation, America's prosecution of the war in Vietnam remains a sensitive issue. Though we may still await a balanced and comprehensive account of America's strategies and actions in the Vietnam war, it is not too soon to point out some of the ways in which that war affected our development assistance policies.

In the first place, development assistance came to be dominated by Vietnam itself. By 1966, that one country was receiving over 43 percent of AID's world-wide development grants,[15] and a similar proportion of AID's talent, energy, and personnel was being applied to problems in Vietnam. The war, moreover, prompted a drastic change in the understanding of what development aid was all about. A violence-rent agrarian society, in which broad stretches of terrain were under the shifting control of contesting armies, was hardly suitable ground for the sort of technical assistance and private investments that the Point Four program had sought to encourage. Development policies had to be adapted, and on the spot; the mutations that evolved had little to do with self-sustaining growth or any of the other desiderata of an earlier generation of technical assistance policies.

As the war proceeded, AID was drawn into such efforts as the "strategic hamlet" and the "civilian relocation" programs. While these may have served a justifiable military purpose, their economic results were almost the exact opposite of development—at least as that word had previously been understood. By feeding, clothing, and housing villagers who had been dispossessed from areas turned into "free-fire zones," the United States maintained, and often improved, their material living standards, but the economic base that might sustain these people was simultaneously being destroyed.

In subordinating economic objectives to military ones, AID exposed itself to the charge of "waste." In a technical sense, such allegations were valid—and, indeed, had to be. The criteria for running a war and running a business are fundamentally at odds. Military effort is judged by its effectiveness in securing objectives; the economic efficiency of subsidiary operations is at most a secondary consideration, and the concept of productivity is, strictly speaking, irrelevant.

There was a greater, more comprehensive problem in Vietnam, which affected aid and everything else the American government was attempting. This was the notorious "credibility gap" separating our actual intentions, policies, and actions in Vietnam from the official descriptions of them. In allowing this gap to develop, the government encouraged the perception that our policies were considered illegitimate by the very men who were framing them. This could only have painful and continuing reverberations in a nation where domestic support for the international application of American power has so typically hinged on the moral purpose implicit in the initiative.

As distrust between the executive and the legislative branches deepened over the conduct of the war, foreign aid became a battleground for a most unfortunate sort of guerrilla warfare. Frustrated by the direction of foreign policy in general, Congress resolved to restrict the government's ability to move economic policy in any direction whatsoever. Within Congress a tactical coalition arose between the "left" (against the war) and the "right" (against waste); separated by most issues, these two forces united in their hostility to foreign aid. They did not kill AID, but in retrospect, what they did do might have been worse.

By denying AID "obligational carryover authority," or the right to keep the use of money it had not committed by the end of the fiscal year; by subjecting AID to a process known as "congressional notification," which required the agency to produce two detailed budgets a year for congressional inspection and in effect gave Congress a line-item veto over even comparatively small projects; and by requiring legalistic impact statements—often as many as seventy-five—for even modest projects within programs, Congress severely restricted the ability of the agency to engage in development and forced AID administrators and project officers to shift their attention from the success of their efforts in the field to the success of their entreaties on the Hill. Sparing AID its institutional life, Congress guaranteed that the organization would be severely and permanently crippled.

The Effect of the Reforms of 1973

The efforts to paralyze AID were symptoms of a broader problem of the Vietnam and post-Vietnam era: American foreign policies had come to lack legitimacy in the eyes of a substantial portion of Congress and the public. A period of groping and confusion had begun, during which America's foreign economic policies in general, and foreign aid policies in particular, broke away from the bipartisan principles that had been established in the early postwar years at a speed that sometimes suggested free fall. The events that derailed our foreign aid policies were specific and discrete; yet in retrospect they seem to form a single, continuing chain of practical and moral errors.

In 1971 and 1972 President Nixon's foreign aid proposals were defeated in Congress; funding for them was arranged only through a catch-all "continuing resolution" at the end of each session. To restore congressional confidence in the foreign aid program, and in the presidential purposes behind it, a new code for American development programs was worked out. These were written into law in the Foreign Assistance Act of 1973 and the Mutual Development and Cooperation Act of the same year. At the time, these acts were described as a compromise. They read today as something very different.[16]

The Foreign Assistance Act of 1973 states as directly as such legislation can that our postwar policies toward poorer regions had been a failure: "The conditions which shaped the United States foreign-assistance program in the past have changed. . . . [O]ur relations with the less developed countries must be revised to reflect these realities." The problem, it was suggested, was that the strategy of export-oriented, self-sustaining growth, which we had advocated since the 1940s, did not actually benefit the common people of the countries it transformed: in the words of the Mutual Development and Cooperation Act, "economic growth does not necessarily lead to social advancement by the poor."

The Foreign Assistance Act implied that American power abroad had been secured through alliances with local leaders who had little interest in the welfare of their own public. Hence, the new American approach to foreign aid "should be . . . targeted on the basics"—meaning that it should be judged by its direct and immediate impact on the living standards of the poorest strata of the recipient nations: "Through the restructured program the United States would be telling the developing countries . . . 'Do not forget the immediate needs of your poorest people.'"

The "reforms of 1973" had sweeping consequences for American development efforts. In establishing "basic human needs" as the ultimate arbiter by which development would be judged, they shifted the purpose of AID from assisting self-sustaining growth to affecting living standards through emergency-style distribution of outside food, medicine, clothing, and materials for shelter. These "basic human needs" stipulations came on top of the operational restrictions already imposed on AID, with their implicit bias against development proposals with deferred benefits or with consequences principally measured in efficiency or productivity.

Thus, American bequests increasingly came to be seen as a means of facilitating a steady flow of funds to the governments of less-developed countries for use in whatever purposes they might choose. Although AID administrators could argue that their grants were "tied" to various purposes or conditions, local leaders generally understood the simple truth that, once received, government revenues were fungible—transferable from one objective to the next—and that aid bequests would become all the more fungible when meant to be applied to an operating budget.

There was a final notable aspect of the legislation of 1973: the explicit purpose of development assistance programs was rewritten in a seemingly slight but nonetheless significant way. Provision 102(a) of the Foreign Assistance Act of 1967 had read: "Development is primarily the responsibility of the people of the less developed countries themselves." In the 1973 legislation, the equivalent passage read, "Development planning must be the responsibility of each sovereign nation." With this semantic change, America was retreating from the concepts of economic health and self-sustaining growth and implicitly repudiating the notion that international markets and free flows of private capital should serve as the instruments by which people might raise themselves to mass affluence. Instead, we had come to endorse, and seemingly to require of recipients of our aid, adherence to the very system of comprehensive planning that our leaders had decried as inimical to the interests of poor peoples scarcely twenty years earlier.

The "reforms of 1973" (also known as the "New Directions" legislation) may yet be hard to evaluate fully, but it is clear that they have had at least one effect. Before Vietnam, the United States could point to a number of self-reliant and prospering economies—Greece, Taiwan, and South Korea among them—that had "graduated" out of American development aid. Since the "reforms of 1973," there have been no new graduates.

The McNamara Era

The decoupling of American development assistance from the policies that had previously been regarded as the best means for improving the economic health of poor nations also bespoke a loss of faith in the

United States. It was no longer naturally assumed that American interests and preferences, pursued in practical fashion, would benefit the peoples of the world. To serve the weak and helpless of the earth, Americans were now advised to restrain themselves and their impulse to international action. The United States was urged instead to assist with the one thing it had that poor governments manifestly lacked: money.

As American-administered development programs took on the trappings of relief work and as the terms "development aid" and "reparations" came to be used interchangeably (in 1973 Nixon administration officials had secretly discussed postwar "development aid" proposals with Hanoi), there arose simultaneously a tendency to give aid through international institutions rather than channeling it directly from our government to the beneficiary capital. Through "multilateralization," it was argued, donor "pressure" on recipient governments might be made to diminish, even as aid outlays were made to rise.

The multilateralization of aid was made easier by the impressive growth of the World Bank under Robert McNamara, the former U.S. secretary of defense who had left the Defense Department around the time of the Tet offensive to assume the bank's presidency. As admirers testified at his retirement in 1981, he oversaw a tenfold increase in the bank's annual commitments. McNamara accomplished this remarkable feat by reinterpreting the bank's mission and its operating rules.

The bank's Articles of Agreement specify that bank funds must be used for "productive investment"; they neglect, however, to qualify the sorts of spending that may be *labeled* productive investment. McNamara took command of the definition of the term. A growing body of economic research was detailing the connection among education, productive knowledge, and economic growth; the results suggested that augmenting "human capital" was as integral to economic development as was deepening the base of "physical capital." McNamara used this research to argue that health, nutrition, education, family planning, and other social services were in fact investments and thus legitimate avenues for the application of bank funds.

While the prerogative for lending was being expanded, the standards for evaluating loans were simultaneously being relaxed. McNamara outlined the bank's new view of lending in 1970: "What contributes the most to the development of the borrowing country should be the decisive factor in both Bank and IDA operations. . . . Any policy which can be justified for IDA as consistent with its development function can, I believe, be equally justified for the Bank, and the Bank itself should adopt it."[17] Since IDA was in the business of dispensing "soft" loans— "of doubtful validity," as David Baldwin pointed out nearly twenty years ago, "by any measured banking standard"[18]—a large pool of capital was being declared exempt from the scrutiny that private loans must customarily withstand.

McNamara's efforts to expand the bank's financial involvement in less-developed countries, while relinquishing some of the rights (and obligations) traditionally assumed to be incumbent on portfolio managers, were consistent, in some ways, with his view of the problems facing the poor nations and the world. Like many of his contemporaries in Congress, McNamara felt that international development efforts had largely failed the poor. As he told the delegates of UNCTAD III in Santiago, Chile, in 1972: "Development programs have been directed largely at gross economic goals, and have failed to insure that all nations, and all groups within nations, have shared equitably in economic advance."[19] The bank's new "basic human needs" (or "social investment") programs were informed by that opinion.

McNamara had decided that an ongoing "global transfer" of public funds would be necessary to meet the problem of world poverty. In his words, "the rich countries have a responsibility to assist the less developed nations. It is not a sentimental question of philanthropy. It is a straightforward issue of social justice."[20] The idea of unconditional concessionary transfers from Western people to low-income governments was echoed and amplified by a number of officials who rose to prominence in the bank during the McNamara years; they gave form to McNamara's more vaguely stated notion through their support of "global negotiations" for the expanded and unrestricted transfer of money from the governments of the "North" to the governments of the "South."

Like many other large institutions, the World Bank has never spoken with a single voice or acted as if by a single hand. Nevertheless, the change in direction during the McNamara years was unmistakable: the felt obligation to provide money to poor nations was growing; the right to monitor its disbursement was more and more open to question. The World Bank had come a long way from the Bretton Woods conference, when Secretary Morgenthau introduced it to the world with these words: "The chief purpose of the International Bank for Reconstruction and Development is to guarantee private loans made through the usual investment channels."[21]

Some observers have seen in McNamara's initiatives at the World Bank a sort of expiation for presumed pangs of conscience over his prosecution of the war in Vietnam as secretary of defense. A less sentimental and more straightforward interpretation might be that the McNamara initiatives simply formalized, and globalized, the new development policies that the United States had experimented with in Vietnam. In any event, the two were characterized by the same effort at divorcing the living standards of national populations from the productive base that would ordinarily be expected to sustain them.

The United Nations as Donor

The multilateral institution that most effectively divorced development funding from the "pressures" of donors, however, was not the World Bank but the United Nations. The story of what happened in, and to, the United Nations over the past two decades is by now a familiar tale. During the 1960s, a voting bloc began to form that defined itself by opposition to American policies in Vietnam. It soon became clear that this bloc was opposed not simply to America's war in Vietnam but to American purposes in the world generally and to the very idea that America should be a country wielding international power. A psychological barrier was crossed in 1970, when this bloc—self-described as "nonaligned"—succeeded in outvoting the United States and its allies on an Albanian resolution to recognize Beijing rather than Taipei as the legitimate seat of Chinese government.[22] Thereafter, the bloc grew, both in numbers and boldness, until it became the decisive force in framing UN policy.

The apparatus of development organizations

erected beneath the UN flag was inevitably influenced by the new thinking in the General Assembly. It had often been said that the International Labor Organization, the UN Educational, Scientific, and Cultural Organization, and the host of other UN agencies became "politicized" in the 1970s; it would be more accurate, however, to say that they simply became suffused with a *new* political ethos—one which, as it happened, was hostile to the meanings of the UN Charter, to the previous purposes of the organization, and to the principles of the Western peoples who provided most of the UN's money.

The UN's new agenda followed largely from the same line of thought that led to the accusation—enunciated by President Salvador Allende of Chile before the same UNCTAD audience where McNamara professed the failure of Western-sponsored development efforts—that the industrial nations had created a world where "the toil and resources of the poorer nations pay for the prosperity of the affluent peoples."[23] In logical fashion, and in strikingly consistent measure, the new development initiatives emanating from the UN were aimed at disassembling the liberal international economic order and in augmenting instead the capacity of states and the authority of their leaders to plan their local economies and to direct their people's societies—and to pay for these therapies with renewed "global transfers" of tax revenues from the Western nations that had supposedly made the cures necessary in the first place.

Although there was little intellectual or (in the strict sense of the word) economic merit in most of the new thoughts circulating through the UN during the 1970s, it must be remembered that Western nations put very little pressure on advocates of the New

International Economic Order to think more clearly or act more decently. The acquiescence of the United States was especially striking. For seven years—from 1970 to 1977—America made virtually no concerted effort to come to the defense of either its national interests or its principles in any of the UN's many forums. (The attempts of Daniel P. Moynihan, in his brief eight-month tenure as ambassador, to force a government response to the anti-American invective by then commonplace at the UN, stood in contrast to the accepted policy of the day but did not alter it.)

America did not lack a foreign policy during the early 1970s. On the contrary, from 1970 to 1977 American foreign policy was more fully controlled, and more intricately directed, than it had ever been before, or has been since. Although Secretary of State Henry Kissinger privately—and occasionally publicly—disagreed with the UN's new development thrusts, he seemed to have felt that they were best parried through accommodation. His major speech on development issues, an address to the General Assembly in 1975, highlighted his general attitude. In the course of his exposition he made many references to the need to strengthen free and competitive international markets, but he also proposed a new concessionary window at the International Monetary Fund from which only third world nations might draw loans and which would allow for the conversion of these IMF loans into "grants under prescribed conditions."[24] Such plans could only diminish considerably the IMF's ability to lobby credibly for economic responsibility with those nations that applied to it for loans; they were also bound to stimulate international inflation at a time when global inflation was already punishing rich countries and poor alike.

Kissinger also proposed new "bilateral support

for training and technical assistance to help developing countries find and exploit new sources of fossil fuel"—a striking suggestion from a U.S. secretary of state, considering that the greatest technical capacities for oil exploration and development resided in the American energy companies then being nationalized throughout the third world. He further recommended—less than two years after the politicization of oil prices by the OPEC cartel—that "a producer-consumer forum be established for every big commodity," the inevitable result of which would be to sanction the setting of commodity prices by political contrivance rather than economic demand.

For the poor countries in the meantime, there were no special offers to aid them in learning the ways of the world's markets; there was, however, plenty of help should they experience the usual side-effects of "development planning": a guaranteed disbursement of 10 million tons of food aid a year; a new IMF facility for "emergency" balance-of-payments problems; and "population assistance" to "help curb demographic growth" and thereby, presumably, take pressure off the economic structure to produce efficiently.

In the United Nations, as in so many other arenas, Kissinger presumably hoped to throw his opponents off guard by agreeing to their demands in principle and then to win the day by rear-guard negotiating tactics. This ploy, however, is considerably less effective when the issue at stake is the principles themselves.

The Carter Presidency

The period of drift and decline in American policies toward the world's poor continued under President

Jimmy Carter. Elected in 1976 on a campaign promise to restore moral purpose to American politics,
Carter seemed to find it extremely difficult in practice
to determine whether any use at all of American
power overseas was in fact moral. The administration's sensitivity to criticism on this score and its am-
bivalence about American purpose were highlighted
in its foreign aid policies.

The administration enthusiastically embraced
the 1973 "reforms," with their seeming evidence that
America was interested in directly aiding the world's
poor. It created the International Development Cooperation Agency (IDCA)—an umbrella organization
above USAID—to remove development assistance
programs from the direct chain of command within
the State Department and thus to shield the United
States from charges that it was using foreign aid to
further America's purposes of state. It agreed to a
continuing cutback in military and security assistance,
since (it was argued) that money might be used for
questionable or even inhumane purposes by our
chosen allies.

The Carter administration also commissioned
two major studies of world poverty. The first, the
Presidential Commission on World Hunger, warned
of "the continuing deterioration of the world food
situation."[25] It stated that "corporations badly undercut efforts to alleviate hunger and malnutrition," and
equivocated about the extent to which international
trade might help reduce hunger. Rather, the report
explained, "redirecting income from the rich to the
poor" would be a principal vehicle for reducing hunger in poor nations, and foreign aid could figure
importantly in this process. Among the recommendations of the commission were a "total" debt for-

47

giveness for the "poorest" developing countries, an easing of IMF lending conditions, an immediate doubling of U.S. development outlays, an increase in Food for Peace authorizations and a relaxation of the conditions for disbursing such produce, the promotion of a UN code to regulate international businesses operating in less-developed countries, and the establishment of a public organization in the United States to lobby for these goals.

The second study, the "Global 2000" report,[26] warned of an impending and generalized series of environmental problems born of overly rapid population growth in the less-developed countries and excessive economic growth in the affluent nations. One implication of this computer-model study was that the sort of sustained economic advancement that would be necessary to draw the world's poor countries out of mass poverty might seriously destabilize the fragile global ecosystem, possibly causing ruin for all. By seeming to question the feasibility of continuing economic growth, "Global 2000" led some observers to conclude that the only viable way to assist poor nations was through the transfer of existing wealth from the Western states.

Without fully realizing it, the Carter administration had thus ended up accepting as counsel in dealing with the less-developed countries many of the basic tenets of the UN's proposed New International Economic Order. What did not seem to be entirely understood was that the New International Economic Order was a call for the liquidation of the liberal international economic order that America had helped to create, and continued to lead.

The Reagan Presidency

Ronald Reagan's decisive victory over President Carter in 1980 seemed to presage more than just a shift in attitudes toward the use of American power on the international scene. The Reagan administration came into office with an articulated and internally consistent vision of America's political and economic role in the world. This vision had implications not only for the international political struggle between the United States and the Soviet Union but also for American policies toward the world economy and toward development.

President Reagan's critics were quick to brand him a reactionary; there was some accuracy in this characterization, albeit inadvertent. More than any president in a generation, Ronald Reagan explicitly embraced the precepts that had guided the foreign economic policies of Presidents Roosevelt and Truman. He emphasized this return to earlier principles in a major speech on international economic development in Philadelphia in October 1981.

"Economic health" was the theme underlying the president's prescriptions for promoting international advancement. There was, he said, a "need to revitalize the U.S. and the world economy as a basis for the social and economic progress of our own and other nations." At the same time, there was "a need for a clearer focus on the real meaning of development and our development record." "The postwar economic system," he asserted, "was created on the belief that the key to national development and human progress is individual freedom—both political and economic."

President Reagan identified five principles by which development might be encouraged:

First, stimulating international trade by opening up markets, both within and between countries. . . .

Second, tailoring particular development strategies to the specific needs and potential of individual countries. . . .

Third, guiding assistance toward the development of self-sustaining productive capacities. . . .

Fourth, improving in many countries the climate for private investment. . . .

Fifth, creating a political atmosphere in which practical solutions can be moved forward—rather than founder on a reef of misguided policies that restrain and interfere with the international marketplace or foster inflation.[27]

Development assistance, in the president's vision, was to be put to the service of these principles. He promised to "work to strengthen the World Bank and other international institutions" and pledged to make available American technical know-how, food, and money "toward the development of self-sustaining productive activities" in poor nations. The president's words suggested that a dramatic change—or more properly, a historic restoration—of American policies was under way.

The Reagan administration's actions, however, suggested something quite different. Instead of bringing America's foreign aid policies back into alignment with the goals and ideals that had originally animated them under Roosevelt and Truman, the Reagan administration allowed American programs to continue down the path charted in the 1970s. So smooth, in fact, was the trajectory that it would be difficult to tell which administration was in power from the statements and actions of its development apparatus. No less than during the Carter years, American development programs under Reagan seemed to be at systematic variance with the objectives of the international order we nominally supported. The administrators of these programs, moreover, appeared increasingly intent upon concealing the discrepancy from the American public.

The Direction of AID

The principal spokesman for the Reagan administration's development program was its acting director of IDCA and administrator of AID, M. Peter McPherson. McPherson made clear his perspective in his first presentation before the House Foreign Affairs Committee in 1981. "We have learned," he said, "that continued progress in Third World development is of growing importance to our own domestic and international well-being. In the past year, public awareness of our interdependence has been highlighted by the Presidential Commission on World Hunger, the Brandt Commission [a panel of inquiry, created by Robert McNamara and headed by former Chancellor Willy Brandt of West Germany, that advocated "massive" and "automatic" transfers of revenue from Western governments to "Southern" states] and the 'Global 2000' study."[28] Embracing the findings of these reports, he instructed the congressional committee on their significance: "Failure to make acceptable progress in ameliorating conditions of poverty can only lead to domestic instability and increasing frustration

51

on the part of Third World governments over the
workings of the international system and the distribution of economic and institutional power in that system as it is now constituted." To observers of the
North-South "dialogue," the device of wrapping a
request for aid in a veiled threat may have been familiar, but in the deliberations between appointed repre-
sentatives of the executive branch and elected repre-
sentatives of the American people this procedure was
something quite new. It had not been seen under
President Carter.

To move American development programs back
to the stimulation of "self-sustaining productive capacities," as the president had pledged, it would have
been necessary to challenge the "New Directions" legislation of the 1970s. AID made no effort to do so.
Two years into his appointment, and again before the
House Foreign Affairs Committee, McPherson may
have suggested why. Reflecting on the early 1970s, he
remarked:

> The political, social, and economic structure
> which had evolved in many less developed coun-
> tries had produced little improvement in eco-
> nomic well-being for the poor of those countries.
> To help correct this situation, a new concern with
> the effects of our assistance on the poor majority
> emerged a decade ago, in the form of the current
> New Directions legislation [of 1973].[29]

This was an implicit endorsement, not only of the
legislation but of the analysis that had prompted it.
That analysis, of course, held that the postwar order
America had created could not be relied upon to
advance the interests of the world's poor.

In 1983, in an aid request, McPherson told Congress that "trade and debt pressure is particularly serious for stability and longer-run economic progress in the low-income countries. . . . Our foreign-assistance program can play an important role in their recovery."[30] It was a revealing analysis. The problems to which he referred were both financial (relating to balance-of-payments shortfalls) and short-term (being exacerbated by a presumably cyclical drop in international economic activity). But development programs, as generally imagined, involve technical transfers and long-term horizons. A development program could play an important role in a short-term economic recovery only if it were intended to infuse money directly into a pool of current spending.

AID's presentations left little doubt about the agency's view of the propriety of direct budgetary transfers. An AID policy paper on health assistance, for example, noted that "by 1982, one half of the Agency's development assistance budget for health supported the delivery of basic health services in LDCs."[31] Such "development-assistance" is, necessarily, a direct bequest from the U.S. Treasury, applied to the operating revenues of recipient states. Whatever may be said of such charitable donations, they are in no sense "self-sustaining."

Confusion over the distinction between recurrent expense and productive investment likewise marked AID's agricultural program. The agency's fiscal year 1983 presentation to Congress proposed to increase agricultural productivity in the less-developed countries through the following activities:

> supporting land tenure arrangements and agrarian reform policies; encouraging small farmer

organizations and local participation; disseminating and developing new technologies; protecting the environmental and natural resource base through better land management; halting and reversing deforestation by developing renewable energy alternatives to firewood, testing fast-growing tree species, and supporting woodlots for fuel; increasing the availability of water, improved seed, credit, and other agricultural inputs at reasonable prices; reducing post-harvest food losses; and facilitating small-farmer access to market.[32]

In this conspectus of agricultural productivity, only one item seemed to be missing: any mention of the prices paid to producers. Yet it is prices, unfortunately, which often prove decisive in the success or failure of agricultural development, determining as they do the returns that may be derived from increasing production or adopting innovations.

The president had suggested that misguided policies played an important role in perpetuating poverty in the less-developed regions; his AID administrator expressed a very different view. In 1983, McPherson told Congress that "the critical problem of excessive population growth in the Third World . . . constitutes the primary obstacle to increasing per capita food production, reducing malnutrition and chronic disease, and conserving dwindling nonrenewable resources."[33] This formulation, with its implication that parents in less-developed nations irrationally choose "excessive" numbers of children, could be understood as excusing governments in those nations from responsibility for agricultural difficulties, hunger problems, or the management of natural resources. It also appeared to lend legitimacy to governmental efforts to control population growth.

AID had maintained that it would condone only voluntary family planning. But even as a position paper to this effect was being circulated publicly, the agency was participating in a $50-million grant to China from the UN Fund for Population Activities. China was pursuing a population campaign known as the "one child norm," requiring parents to agree to have only a single offspring. The campaign appears to have been horribly unpopular with the overwhelming majority of the Chinese people, and the Chinese government found it necessary to use pressure, threats, far-reaching punishments against married couples to enforce the decree.[34] (Many infant girls and able-bodied women are thought to have died as a result of this program.[35]) Since most of the funding in which AID participated was earmarked for Chinese "population education activities" and for health clinics (at which quotas of sterilizations and abortions were being fulfilled in accordance with the population plan), it would have required extreme mental agility to dissociate the Reagan administration's development money from the practice of involuntary population control.

Still another area in which AID seemed to disagree with received American policy was on the issue of private enterprise. AID is committed by law to refrain from using its funds to displace private investment or private commercial activity. Despite this, AID's 1983 budget presentation before Congress stated that, since energy "has become a field of major concern to AID," the agency had "increasingly broadened its assistance to encompass technical assistance to expand indigenous supplies of coal, oil, and gas."[36]

The projects involved were not described, but it would seem difficult to reconcile these activities with AID's legal mandate.

The question of private enterprise and its legitimate scope within development seems to have troubled AID administrators deeply during the Reagan years. One attempt to resolve the issue was the creation of a Bureau of Private Enterprise. In a sense, however, this only compounded the problem: for the first time in its history, AID was formally and explicitly separating the job of encouraging private commerce from its overall responsibilities in promoting development. Moreover, the private enterprise initiative did not have enthusiastic AID backing. In its heyday it was allocated $27 million; since then, its funding has declined. Although no other program receives such extensive coverage in AID's annual budget presentation before Congress, the private enterprise initiative now accounts for something less than one-half of 1 percent of AID's expenditures.

Recently, it is true, AID statements and publications have begun to express formal support for the liberal international economic order. But if the tone has changed, AID's priorities have not. In 1984, a top-level internal document on strategy and objectives for a second Reagan term proposed that AID's mission be redefined to include the following goals: the raising of life expectancy in all developing countries to over sixty years, the reduction of infant-mortality rates in all developing countries to 75 per 1,000 or below, and the increase to 70 percent of literacy rates in all developing countries.[37] As the draft noted, this change in mandate would require a "renewal" in America's commitment to development funding; indeed, to follow through on such a program in a world where recipient governments maintain sovereign authority over their economic and social policies, this renewed commitment would have to be not only major but virtually open ended.

This internal AID document contains a number of formal concessions to the notions of "self-sustaining growth" and "policy reform." Yet as it was outlined, AID's plan for promoting development would not emphasize policies to create self-sustaining growth or to encourage conditions by which living standards might undergo an internally generated transformation; it would, rather, concentrate on the direct and restitutive redress of poverty through social spending. If the rhetoric of the Carter commissions and the Brandt commission had been carefully airbrushed out of AID's public statements in the 1984 election year, such thinking was still clearly acceptable in the inner recesses of the Reagan administration's development apparatus.

Foreign Aid in El Salvador

It may be useful to conclude with a look at the effect of recent American foreign aid policies on a single nation: El Salvador.[38]

To be sure, even by the variegated standards of the developing nations, El Salvador's problems are not typical. Among other things, the country is caught in a bloody war between government forces and Communist-supported troops, a war that has resulted in both severe destruction and massive emigration from this little land. But it is precisely the exceptional quality of El Salvador's circumstances as a small country that needs American help badly, is receptive to American advice, and is the object of a major strategic and financial commitment that makes it an illuminating case for the study of American foreign aid efforts in general.

El Salvador is, first and foremost, a country at war. Economic development is unlikely to proceed there unless civil order is restored, so that a climate free of undue physical risk to investment and commerce may assert itself. Such problems would seem to be best addressed by security assistance. The Reagan administration, however, has been extremely cautious in extending military aid to El Salvador, preferring to restrict it to a plausible minimum while increasing quite freely the funding for development assistance and economic support. As late as 1983 two years into the Reagan administration's escalated commitment to El Salvador, the ratio of development to military aid for that nation was on the order of 3:1—this, at a time when American military advisers in El Salvador were explicitly asserting that the security-assistance bequests were inadequate for the tasks at hand.

That is a highly problematic approach. In the midst of war, investments in infrastructure or American-sponsored local projects are unlikely to promise high rates of return, especially since the projects themselves may well become targets for destruction or disruption by guerrilla forces. By the same token, economic support to cover balance-of-payments problems would seem ill-suited to the difficulties stemming from such symptoms of wartime deterioration as capital flight and the destruction of export industries.

Constraining military aid during a state of war— providing some, but not enough to win—can only be considered a false economy. Providing economic aid *instead of* military aid in wartime makes still less sense.

Such bequests may cushion the decline in living standards that fighting, disruption, and uncertainty inevitably bring, but they are unlikely either to bring fighting to an end or to restore the political stability upon which self-sustaining growth must ultimately rest.

American economic aid to El Salvador has necessarily addressed the problem of feeding and providing for refugees, as it did in Vietnam. Under emergency conditions such bequests serve both political and humanitarian ends, although they make little contribution to development as such. But AID was also involved in programs to bring long-term economic change to El Salvador, foremost among them land reform.

After the coup against the old oligarchy in 1979, El Salvador's new junta determined upon a major redistribution of the nation's heretofore highly concentrated land holdings. This program was to be a sort of "land to the tiller" reform. The large plantations would be broken into small parcels to be owned by the *hacenderos* who had worked them; in smaller estates ownership would eventually devolve on those who had farmed the fields. In this way, it was thought, El Salvador's farmers might be converted from landless tenants and day laborers into a class of landowners—possibly even into a middle class.

AID involved itself in these reforms at the Salvadoran government's request under President Carter and seemed to take an even more prominent role under the Reagan administration. The plan for "Phase III" of El Salvador's land reform (which was to give title to some 60,000 families from the smaller estates) was drawn up by American consultants and paid for by the Reagan administration. True, legislation sponsored by Senator Jesse Helms prevented the administration from paying directly for El Salvador's land reform by prohibiting the use of aid money for compensation of confiscated agricultural or banking enterprises. In practice, however, such strictures had little effect on the land reform program, given the realities of fungibility at a time when American aid was rapidly increasing.

To Americans, the phrase "land reform" often evokes images from our own agrarian past. But the policies America supported and promoted in El Salvador bore little correspondence to the Homestead Act. El Salvador's first step to land reform was the creation of the Salvadoran Institute for Agrarian Transformation. This institute expropriated the nation's large plantations, compensating former owners with government bonds that could not be redeemed until the end of the century and then only at their nominal face value, unadjusted for intervening inflation. The deeds from these estates, moreover, were not turned over to individual peasants or their families; instead, the land was deeded directly to newly formed "cooperatives," certified by the institute. With no title of their own, peasants could not sell their holdings or transfer their interest to a different cooperative. Voluntary association was thus impossible; a peasant's only options under the new system were to remain with his cooperative or to move and forfeit everything.

With no title of his own, the new "landowner" also could not raise credit against his holdings. Credit was only to be raised by the cooperative's management committee and was to be allocated as the management committee determined. A peasant's chances of receiving credit thus depended largely on his role in fulfilling the plan that the management committee drew up. Since each committee had a representative of the government on its board and since credit was now allocated to the cooperative by the central government, the new arrangements made *hacenderos* more sensitive to agricultural directives from the capital than they had ever been in the past.

The title program for the smaller estates, the so-called Phase III of land reform, was also managed by the Salvadoran Institute for Agrarian Transformation. As with the hacienda reforms, title to land did not devolve clearly and directly to the peasants. Once arrangements were settled (and this itself often proved a long and difficult matter), peasants would obtain an eventual title to their parcel—so long as the head of the household continued to live and farm on it for the next thirty years. In the meantime they would not be able to raise credit from it through secondary mortgages; if the head of the household were to move or die in the intervening thirty years, "his" land would go not to his family but back to the institute.

The perverse effects of the new land reforms were soon apparent. On cooperatives, peasants petitioned for the right to grow vegetables in "private plots" and to rent the land they nominally owned so that they might farm it according to their own practices rather than the directives of the management committee. On the smaller holdings, peasants were in effect frozen to their land. Both land reforms had forgotten to take into account the fact that El Salvador was a society with an active rural labor market, in which peasants had moved through their small nation in pursuit of seasonal employment.[39] The new arrangements and their attendant uncertainties virtually precluded "landowners" from pursuing what had previously been an important source of family income. The new arrangements also tended to restrict the healthy growth of towns and rural industries, whose markets and products had typically proved important in countries that had undergone successful rural development.

One perverse effect led to another. The new land policies could not be enforced or financed without controlling the availability of credit. The Salvadoran government thus found it necessary early on to nationalize the country's private banks. Since the private banks were, by one estimate, custodians of some 40 percent of the nation's credit portfolio, the government also nationalized much of the nation's industry in the process. AID did not protest.

When El Salvador's Central Reserve Bank was established in the 1930s, David Raynolds has noted, "the basic law regulating its functions carefully provided that the national government could not hold stock in the bank, since it was feared that otherwise the credit function would become subject to political manipulation."[40] Under the new arrangement, all formal credit was controlled by the government. Interest rates were set considerably below the rate of inflation. This made loans a gift; not surprisingly, loans were increasingly dispensed in the way that gifts tend to be. The Reagan administration did not object to this. Questioned before Congress on the administration's support of an IMF loan to El Salvador in 1982, Richard Erb, U.S. representative to the IMF, argued that "there is not a rigid [IMF] criteria [sic] that there should be a positive real interest rate."[41] Legally, he was correct; yet it is difficult to overlook the consequences of such a posture, either for the

Salvadoran economy or on the bargaining positions of the many poorer countries that were to attempt to negotiate IMF loans in the early and mid-1980s.

Each control required another. To check inflation, price controls were enforced; to compensate for the loss in international competition, foreign exchange controls were imposed; to make up for the loss in governmental export revenues, mechanisms were created to purchase cash crops at unusually low prices from the cooperatives. All these controls had the inevitable effect of eroding business confidence; domestic capital continued its flight abroad; the economy listed further into decline.

A strange new form of poverty seemed to be settling over El Salvador, not entirely related to the destruction of war. The destruction now becoming evident was one underwritten by government policies. These policies were not only supported by Washington; in some cases they were recommended by Washington. And in all cases, ultimately, they were funded by Washington.

The Cost of Failure

The record of the past decades shows, in sum, that America's foreign aid policies are in trouble—not because the American people lack compassion for the suffering of others overseas and not because Americans are unwilling to devote their nation's resources to helping other peoples but because the policies themselves are formulated and implemented in such a way as to suggest that the United States no longer understands the nature of the problems facing poor people and poor countries. Far from contributing to the goal of self-sustained economic progress in the low-income regions, our funds are instead being directed to a tragic extent into the construction of barriers against such progress and in some cases may actually be paying for the creation of poverty, albeit in new and pernicious variants. This state of affairs can continue only at great human cost to those whom we mean to help—and at great moral cost to our nation.

The cost, indeed, may be more consequential than is commonly appreciated by cool-headed advocates of a "pragmatic" American foreign policy. The experience of the United States in the world arena since the end of World War I suggests that, for our nation more than any other, power and principle are inseparable. When the legitimacy and moral purpose of American initiatives overseas have been commonly understood and accepted, our government has proved able to mobilize awesome resources in the pursuit of its objectives. When, by contrast, the legitimacy and moral purpose of American efforts have become open to question, the domestic base of support has dramatically diminished and with it the possibility of pursuing those efforts with any hope of success.

The premises of the liberal international economic order the United States labored to create from the wreckage of World War II remains valid, and the instruments of this order remain capable of creating extraordinary opportunities for general material advance throughout all regions of the world. The failures of American aid policies in recent decades are a reflection not on the soundness of the conceptions that originally brought these policies to life but rather on the degree to which current practice has become divorced from original purpose. America's foreign aid policies today stand in contradistinction to the thrust and purpose of America's overall foreign policy and to the values and ideals of the American people. How we deal with this contradiction will affect not only the poor and the unprotected of the earth, whose champions we should rightly be, but our own conception of ourselves and our ability to function in the world of nations.

Notes

1. John E. Reilly, ed., *American Public Opinion and U.S. Foreign Policy* (Chicago: Chicago Council on Foreign Relations, 1983).

2. Article I (ii); reprinted in Edward S. Mason and Robert E. Asher, *The World Bank since Bretton Woods* (Washington, D.C.: Brookings Institution, 1973), p. 759.

3. E. M. Bernstein, "A Practical International Monetary Policy," *American Economic Review,* vol. 34, no. 4 (December 1944), p. 782.

4. Mason and Asher, *World Bank since Bretton Woods,* pp. 169–76.

5. *New York Times,* March 27, 1945.

6. February 18, 1945; quoted in David A. Baldwin, *Economic Development and American Foreign Policy, 1943–1962* (Chicago: University of Chicago Press, 1966), p. 13.

7. For a useful overview, see William Adams Brown, Jr., and Redvers Opie, *American Foreign Assistance* (Washington, D.C.: Brookings Institution, 1953), pp. 145–312; see also Ludwig Erhard, *Germany's Comeback in the World Market* (London: George Allen and Unwin, 1954).

8. George C. McGhee, February 27, 1950; cited in Baldwin, *Economic Development and American Foreign Policy,* p. 78.

9. Testimony of Harold Linder before the Subcommittee on Foreign Economic Policy, House Committee on Foreign Affairs, March 12, 1953; Reprinted in U.S. Congress, *Foreign Economic Policy* (Washington, D.C.: 1953), p. 4.

10. February 21, 1946; reprinted in David A. Baldwin, *Foreign Aid and American Foreign Policy* (New York: Frederick A. Praeger, 1966), p. 51.

11. *New York Times,* September 17, 1948.

12. Quoted in Baldwin, *Economic Development and American Foreign Policy,* p. 21.

13. *New York Times,* June 17, 1961.

14. Testimony before the Subcommittee on Foreign Economic Policy, House Committee on Foreign Affairs, April 30, 1953; reprinted in *Foreign Economic Policy,* p. 309.

15. Derived from U.S. Agency for International Development, *U.S. Overseas Loans and Grants and Assistance for International Organizations: Obligations and Authorizations, July 1, 1945–June 30, 1975* (Washington, D.C.: U.S. Agency for International Development, n.d.), pp. 6, 82.

16. This section draws upon Ellen Z. Berg, "The 1973 Legislative Reorientation of the United States Foreign Assistance Policy: The Content and Context of a Change" (Master's thesis, George Washington University, 1976).

17. Robert S. McNamara, "Address to the Board of Governors, Copenhagen, Denmark," September 21, 1970, reprinted in World Bank, *The McNamara Years at the World Bank: Major Policy Addresses of Robert S. McNamara, 1968–1981* (Baltimore, Md.: Johns Hopkins University Press, 1981), p. 117.

18. Baldwin, *Economic Development and American Foreign Policy,* p. 6.

19. "Address to the United Nations Conference on Trade and Development," Santiago, Chile, April 14, 1972, reprinted in World Bank, *The McNamara Years at the World Bank,* p. 171.

20. McNamara, "Address to the Board of Governors," p. 120.

21. Henry Morgenthau, Jr., "Address to the United Nations Monetary and Financing Conference at Bretton Woods," reprinted in Baldwin, *Foreign Aid and American Foreign Policy,* p. 49.

22. Henry A. Kissinger, *The White House Years* (Boston: Little, Brown, 1979), p. 771.

23. Henry A. Kissinger, *Years of Upheaval* (Boston: Little, Brown, 1982), p. 392.

24. Henry A. Kissinger, "Global Consensus and Economic Development," Address to the U.N. General Assembly, Seventh Special Session, September 1, 1975, reprinted in Henry A. Kissinger, *American Foreign Policy* (New York: W. W. Norton, 1977).

25. Presidential Commission on World Hunger, *Overcoming World Hunger: The Challenge Ahead* (Washington, D.C.: 1980).

26. *The Global 2000 Report to the President* (Washington, D.C.: 1980).

27. "Cooperative Strategy for Global Growth," Address before the World Affairs Council in Philadelphia, October 15, 1981; reprinted in Department of State Bulletin, vol. 81, December 1981.

28. "Statement as Acting IDCA Director," House Committee on Foreign Affairs, March 19, 1981; reprinted in *Department of State Bulletin*, vol. 81, May 1981, p. 43.

29. "Statement before the House Budget Committee Task Force on International Finance and Trade," March 2, 1983; reprinted in *Department of State Bulletin*, vol. 83, May 1983, p. 49.

30. Ibid., p. 47.

31. *AID Policy Paper: Health Assistance* (Washington, D.C.: U.S. Agency for International Development, Bureau for Program and Policy Coordination, December 1982), p. 3.

32. *AID Congressional Presentation, Fiscal Year 1983* (Washington, D.C: U.S. Agency for International Development, 1982), p. 20.

33. "Statement before the House Budget Committee," p. 53.

34. John S. Aird, "Coercion in Family Planning: Causes, Methods, and Consequences," in U.S. Congress Joint Economic Committee, *China's Economy Looks toward the Year 2000, vol. 1, The Four Modernizations* (Washington, D.C.: 1986).

35. Ibid.

36. *AID Congressional Presentation*, p. 121.

37. This paper was ultimately published, with only minor revisions, as *Blueprint for Development: The Strategic Plan for the Agency for International Development* (Washington, D.C.: U.S. Agency for International Development, n.d.).

38. The following discussion draws in part upon Claudia Rosett, "Economic Paralysis in El Salvador," *Policy Review,* no. 30 (Fall 1984), and Alvin H. Bernstein and John D. Waghelstein, "How to Win in El Salvador," *Policy Review,* no. 27 (Winter 1984).

39. See, for example, David Browning, *El Salvador: Land and Society* (New York: Oxford University Press, 1971), pp. 252–56. The importance of rural labor markets to the livelihood of El Salvador's rural population was not appreciated by American policy makers in the early 1980s. The topic, for example, is not even mentioned in the *Report of the National Bipartisan Commission*

on Central America (Washington, D.C.: Office of the President, January 1984, also known as the Kissinger Commission), a multi-million dollar document prepared for the president with the express purpose of identifying and providing counsel on both the immediate and the more enduring problems in the area.

40. David R. Raynolds, *Rapid Development in Small Economies: The Example of El Salvador* (New York: Frederick A. Praeger, 1967), p. 71.

41. "Testimony before the Subcommittee on International Trade, Investment, and Monetary Policy of the House Committee on Banking, Finance, and Urban Affairs, August 12, 1982," reprinted in U.S. Congress, *Oversight Hearing on the International Monetary Fund Loan to El Salvador* (Washington, D.C.: 1982), p. 18.

TWO

Famine, Development, and Foreign Aid

In recent years, American foreign aid policies have been shaped increasingly by the argument that the many different problems facing the poor nations are inextricably interconnected, woven together into an all-encompassing "seamless fabric." However pleasing this notion may seem to theoreticians, its practical implications are dangerously wrong. The problems facing poor nations can be distinguished from each other and treated separately—and must be. It is no act of charity to suspend the rules of policy analysis and problem solving at the borders of the third world.

Although current American policies often fail to distinguish among them, three separate purposes underlie our foreign aid programs. The first is the humanitarian purpose of alleviating suffering and minimizing loss of life from the upheavals following sudden, unexpected catastrophe. The second is the developmental purpose of encouraging poor countries to find their best path to economic health, self-sustaining growth, and general prosperity. The third purpose is to promote the security of the United States and the Western order through military aid or security assistance to a foreign government.

Military aid to less-developed countries is but a part of a larger, global American defense strategy. The aid the United States extends to countries that happen to be poor, moreover, is only a tiny fraction of the money it expends to preserve the security of Allied nations that are already rich—such as Japan and the NATO countries. Military aid to less-developed countries, then, is not in any meaningful sense a third world policy, even though it involves transfers of money and resources to nations in the third world.

Humanitarian aid and development aid are quite different. These address, respectively, short-term exigencies and long-term prospects of poor countries and are governed by an attention to poverty. To understand the best use of these different forms of aid, we must appreciate the problems each must address. Let us examine them separately.

Disaster and Famine

Much of mankind continues to live under the shadow of life-imperiling disasters and upheavals. Floods, earthquakes, and storms still endanger millions of people every year, and the human cost of famine is even greater. Since the end of World War II it is believed that tens of millions of people have perished from famine in Asia alone.

To deal effectively with today's natural disasters, we must begin by recognizing that there is very little that is natural about them. Acts of God cannot be prevented, but the quotient of human risk and suffering they exact can be vastly and systematically reduced. Current events underline the point. The United States and Japan happen to be more subject than most regions of the earth to sudden natural disturbances. The Japanese archipelago, after all, is an earthquake zone, buffeted by tropical storms and exposed to *tsunami* (tidal waves). The U.S. land mass is threatened by earthquakes, tropical storms, and tornadoes, and the country, in addition, has more active volcanoes than any other. Nevertheless, very few people in Japan or America die from these natural perils.

The African continent, by contrast, would appear to be comparatively well protected against sudden disasters. It is exposed only slightly to tropical storms and tidal waves, and has only a small earthquake belt and few active volcanoes; it experiences tornadoes only in South Africa. Despite these natural advantages, however, sub-Saharan Africa has been stricken by perennial disaster in the decade since decolonization was effectively completed. These disasters are believed to have cost hundreds of thousands of lives.

Western peoples have not always enjoyed their present protection against adverse acts of nature. In the first ten years of the twentieth century, over 8,000 Americans died in hurricanes,[1] as opposed to the 100 who died over the past ten years. What accounts for this almost 99 percent drop, despite a doubling of the population and a steady urbanization of the coasts where hurricanes most often strike? Affluence, as manifested in safer dwellings, explains part of the change; even more, however, is explained by those handmaidens of affluence, technical advance and government competence. Improvements in com-

71

munications, transportation, weather tracking, emergency management, rescue operations, and relief capabilities have made it possible to reduce dramatically the human price exacted by even the worst hurricanes in the most populated areas. Purposeful private and governmental action can now substantially cut the toll from other natural disasters as well, even in the poorest nations.

Not all governments, however, work at minimizing the havoc that sudden disasters wreak upon their people—as the two most costly sudden disasters of the 1970s attest. In 1970, East Pakistan, as it was then known, was devastated by a typhoon. The Pakistani government—seated in and dominated by West Pakistan—responded to the extreme distress in its Bengal territory with what might at best be described as reserve. As many as 100,000 Bengalis are thought to have perished in the aftermath of that typhoon.[2]

In 1976, the city of Tangshan in China was flattened by an earthquake. One of the Chinese government's first responses to the disaster was to announce it would refuse all international offers of aid for the victims. Details about the actual rescue operations that China itself undertook remain obscure to this day. One of the few accounts of the disaster permitted in the Chinese press at the time was a front-page feature in the *People's Daily* praising a peasant who let his own two children die as he rescued instead an aged party cadre;[3] local and foreign readers came to their own conclusions about what this carefully placed article was intended to suggest. Since the rise of Deng Xiaoping, China's media have severely criticized his predecessors' handling of the Tangshan affair; they now state that almost a quarter of a million people died in the disaster.[4]

If government action can be consequential in limiting the suffering caused by sudden upheavals, it can be even more important in controlling or preventing famine. In the past, famines were typically related to regionalized crop failure. It is now possible to cushion the impact of crop failure in even the poorest regions of the earth. Concerned governments can monitor the progress of their nations' harvests by following local markets, by direct on-site inspection, and by studying the data from worldwide aerial and meteorological surveillance services.

These early-warning systems can give governments valuable months in which to prepare against food shortfalls. Food grain may be purchased from the world market, which trades and transports over 200 million tons each year. If for some reason a government cannot finance its emergency food grain needs, it may draw upon the 7-million-ton reserve of concessional food aid that Western governments set aside each year. If a government lacks the administrative capacity to manage a far-reaching relief effort, it may request free assistance from the many impartial international organizations that have proved they can both supervise and staff effective relief operations on short notice and under difficult conditions. Almost twenty years ago, concerted American-Indian cooperation after a series of harvest failures saved millions of Indians from starvation and seems even to have prevented death rates from rising in the afflicted provinces.[5] Since then, the capabilities of both the world food system and the international relief organizations have grown steadily. They now present even the most modest and least sophisticated government with an opportunity to control famine within its borders—if it wants to do so.

The terrible truth, however, is that many governments in the world today have demonstrated that they are not interested in seeing their people fed. Some have deliberately ignored signs of incipient crisis. Others have interfered with international relief for their stricken groups. Still others have actually created famine conditions through premeditated action. In every recent instance where a potential food shortfall has developed into a mass famine, the hand of the state has been prominently involved.

Consider the great famines that have gripped the poor regions over the past quarter-century. In China, the Three Lean Years lasted from 1959 to 1962. Chinese officials now say that millions of people died during this famine, and Western demographers have recently suggested that "excess mortality" during this period may have been as much as 30 million.[6] The Three Lean Years were a direct consequence of the Great Leap Forward, an awesomely ambitious social and economic experiment that resulted in a nationwide collapse of agriculture and a brief but virtually total destruction of the national food system. Even as their policies were causing millions of their citizens to starve, China's leaders denied there was a crisis, refused all offers of international aid, and exported food.

In Nigeria, where perhaps a million ethnic Ibos died of famine in the late 1960s and early 1970s, the federal government deliberately encouraged starvation in that province, which had proclaimed its independence, in the hope that this would hasten its reconquest.[7] In Ethiopia in the early 1970s, the Haile Selassie regime consciously concealed a famine that was ravaging its minority peoples; it is now said that several hundred thousand people lost their lives as a result of this deception, although the exact cost will never be known.[8] In the mid-1970s, the Indonesian government attacked, occupied, and annexed the territory of East Timor; it used hunger as a weapon of conquest. It is believed by outside observers that over 100,000 Timorese starved to death before Indonesia allowed the island to be fed; in all, as much as a quarter of the Timorese population may have perished from famine.[9] In the late 1970s as many as 2 million Cambodians may have died as a result of hunger; they did so only because the Khmer Rouge government made the mass extermination of whole segments of the national population its official policy.[10]

In the mid-1980s famine struck again in Ethiopia. Although its ultimate toll is yet to be determined, its causes are already apparent. After seizing power in 1974, Ethiopia's Marxist-Leninist Dergue (Armed Forces Coordinating Committee) launched a campaign against "capitalism" in the countryside, restricting and ultimately prohibiting the private sale and marketing of farm produce and agricultural implements. At the same time, a newly formed secret police executed thousands of students and skilled workers in this predominantly illiterate nation, imprisoned tens of thousands more, and caused even greater numbers to flee their homeland.[11] With the encouragement of Soviet and Cuban advisers, the government used its foreign aid to underwrite military buildup and war.

In a country like Ethiopia, which has always been subject to drought, such policies ensured that widespread famine would be only a matter of time. When famine finally did strike, moreover, the Dergue gave little priority to relief efforts. Although millions of its citizens were said to be directly affected by the food shortage, in 1984 the regime concentrated on commemorating its tenth anniversary in power—in a celebration said to have cost the equivalent of over $100 million.

Relief operations do not seem to have begun in earnest until after an outcry in the West over the plight of the famine victims. Even then, the Ethiopian government continued to obstruct international efforts to alleviate its people's distress. Instead of helping rescue workers reach famine victims in Tigre and Wollo—stricken regions where the Dergue is especially unpopular—the government began a program of mass deportations; 2.4 million of those areas' most able-bodied (thus least endangered) people were scheduled for eventual removal. And in contravention of the two basic principles of humanitarian relief—impartiality and nondiscrimination—the *Dergue* forbade all relief for the territory of Eritrea. Half a million people were reported to be starving in Eritrea, but this did not stop the Ethiopian armed forces from attacking convoys suspected of bringing relief supplies into the afflicted region.

Ethiopia is not the only government currently contriving to foment mass starvation. The ongoing efforts of the Soviet Union in Afghanistan, for example, are often forgotten. Since the 1979 invasion, Soviet forces have carefully destroyed the food system in many resisting regions. In so doing, they have turned literally millions of Afghans into destitute refugees, no longer able to feed themselves in their own nation. Over 2 million of these people subsist today in refugee camps in Pakistan. They are kept alive by charity from the West.[12]

The American architects of the postwar international order did not anticipate such problems. In 1943, as President Franklin D. Roosevelt laid the foundations for the broadest and most successful relief effort the world had ever seen, he explained that the new United Nations Relief and Rehabilitation Agency (UNRRA) would be operating only in "liberated areas." He assured "liberated peoples" that "in victory or defeat, the United Nations have never deviated from adherence to the basic principles of freedom, tolerance, independence, and security."[13] President Roosevelt believed that preventing famine would be an eminently manageable task under governments that respected the sanctity of human life and upheld Western values, and he was right. With the spread in membership in the United Nations, moreover, it seemed that enlightened governance might eventually prevail across the entire globe. Today, however, only a handful of countries beyond the borders of the West embrace the values codified in the United Nations' Charter and its Universal Declaration of Human Rights. Many member states now disregard these codes when they prove inconvenient. Others reject them out of principle, since they are inconsistent with their regimes' totalitarian or anti-Western ideologies.

It is now almost forty years since our victory in World War II. Even so, very few of the world's poorest and most vulnerable peoples live in what President Roosevelt would have considered "liberated areas." It is this fact and not any other that accounts for the persistence of famine in the modern world. Countries can always share the West's technical capacities to save people stricken by catastrophe, but regimes that do not share the West's values cannot be counted on to put these capacities to use.

The Magnitude and Impact of Aid

According to many leaders in the third world and to some development organizations in the West, the principal obstacle to accelerating the pace of material progress in low-income nations today is the insufficiency of concessionary aid from Western countries. It is striking, and inadvertently revealing, that such criticisms of Western giving often neglect to discuss either the quality of the aid received or the ends achieved. Such thinking is worse than illogical. By dissociating development aid from measurable results, it reduces Western assistance from a practical policy to an aesthetic, possibly only a symbolic, gesture. To advocate massive new aid programs irrespective of their impact on the economic health of recipient nations would be expensive for the West but could prove far more costly to the world's poor.

Few people in the West appreciate the magnitude of current resource flows from Western societies to the third world. Such flows are, in fact, extremely difficult to measure, not only because of the inevitable delays between commitments and disbursals but because of the complexities of tracking and accounting for funds in a world financial system that is at once open and closed. Nevertheless, the Organization for Economic Cooperation and Development (OECD) attempts to measure these flows, and its computations are instructive.[14] In 1982, the net total for what it labels "overseas development assistance" provided directly by Western nations to third world countries was about $18 billion.

But there was more. Multilateral development banks and multilateral development agencies, underwritten overwhelmingly by Western donations, pro-

78

vided an additional sum whose 1982 net OECD put at about $8 billion. And there was still more. Western nations were also providing finance capital to less-developed countries under a variety of arrangements, including bank lending, government-to-government loans, export credits, and direct private investment. All told, OECD placed the total net transfer of financial resources from Western nations to third world countries at almost $80 billion in 1982. This, it must be emphasized, is supposed to be the *net* total: the residual after financial withdrawals, profit repatriation, and loan repayments have been taken into account.

Of course, 1982 is but a single year. OECD estimates of financial flows to developing countries extend back to 1956. According to these computations, the net transfer of financial resources (both concessional and commercial) from Western nations to less-developed countries between 1956 and 1982 exceeded $670 billion. This figure, however, seriously understates the true magnitude of the transfer, since it is denominated in current rather than in inflation-adjusted dollars. Adjusting for intervening inflation, we find that the OECD estimate would be valued today at over $1,500 billion—that is, over $1.5 *trillion.*

Even this figure, however, understates the total postwar transfer of resources from the West to the third world. It does not, for example, seem to measure either concessional grants or commercial loans for military matters, even though these play a prominent role in the finances of many developing countries. And it obviously cannot measure the net flow of resources in either the first half of the 1950s or the years since 1982. Taking everything into account, it seems quite possible that the total net transfer of capital from the West to the third world since the beginning of the postwar international order may have already exceeded $2 trillion at today's prices. Although the complexities of international financial accounting and the unavoidable inexactitudes of adjusting for inflation and international fluctuations in exchange rates prevent us from arriving at a more precise figure, $2 trillion will probably do as the nearest round number to describe the magnitude of the net financial transfer from the West to the poor nations in the postwar era.

Large figures tend to seem abstract, and $2 trillion is an especially large figure. One way to appreciate its size is to consider what it could buy in 1985. Think of the entire U.S. farm system. Now think of all the industries listed on the New York Stock Exchange. At their market values in 1985, $2 trillion would pay for *both*.

What has been the impact on the societies that have received this extraordinary transfer of Western wealth? The answer is obviously different in every case. Even so, broad and unmistakable patterns arise, some of which can be glimpsed in the composition of the transfers themselves. Less than one quarter of the inflation-adjusted total for the years 1956 to 1982, for example, appears to have accrued from direct (and voluntary) overseas private investment. That fraction, moreover, has steadily diminished over time. Whereas in the late 1950s direct private investment accounted for almost two-fifths of the net financial flows to the less-developed countries, in the five years between 1978 and 1982, OECD figures indicate the fraction has dropped to below one-sixth.

One of the original arguments for foreign aid was that development assistance would increase the capacities of poor countries to make productive use of international investment resources. The record seems to suggest that precisely the opposite has happened. Despite hundreds of billions of dollars of Western development assistance, and a generation of economic growth in the meantime, the less-developed countries, taken as a group, obtain a far smaller fraction of their foreign resources from direct private investment today than they did a quarter of a century ago. This must mean either that third world nations, taken as a group, have grown more hostile to direct private investments or that they have become less capable of attracting such investment, or both.

The eclipse of direct private investment from the West was made possible in no small part by the ascension of an alternative medium of capital transfer, commercial lending. Unlike direct private investment, bank loans to less-developed countries accrue principally to governments and state-owned public corporations. Such lending effectively severed the connection between the provision of capital and the right to manage it. The responsibility for determining the use of these funds, and of repaying them, fell squarely on the state. It was not long before dozens of governments in the third world announced that they would be unable to repay their commercial obligations to their Western creditors on schedule.

The attitudes that led to this generalized debt crisis were highlighted in the subsequent rescheduling negotiations in which many third world governments requested debt relief. Such proposals would have converted a substantial portion of their obligations into a retroactive and unintended gift from the West. This view of Western capital suggested not only that it would be appropriate to convert commercial funds into concessional bequests without warning, but, no less significantly, that there was no reason to expect concessional bequests to earn productive returns.

Within the diverse and disparate amalgam of nations that goes by the name third world there has been a dramatic and general improvement in material living standards during the era of Western transfers. This fact should be neither ignored nor belittled. Life expectancy for the people of "developing regions," according to the World Health Organization, rose by over 50 percent between the late 1930s and the late 1960s, and has risen still further since then.[15] Although no great confidence can be placed in economic estimates for the less-developed regions, the World Bank says that per capita GNP has more than doubled between 1960 and 1980 for the billion people living in what it terms "middle-income economies."[16] According to the same source, per capita GNP rose by over 30 percent in India during this period. Even the most troubled states, the category labeled "other low-income economies" of Africa and Asia, are said to have experienced a 20 percent increase in per capita GNP during these two decades alone.

But while the peoples of the less-developed countries have seen far-reaching material advances in their societies, their economies have also typically undergone strange and troublesome transformations. In a great many countries of the third world it has proved possible to finance the ambitious and comprehensive recasting of the national economy in ways not unlike the mobilizations of societies preparing for protracted and total war. These exercises in economic conversion have left the structures of some less-developed countries grotesquely distorted, unnecessarily incapable of meeting either the social needs or the commercial demands of their people. They have left many others in a curious state of economic imbalance: richer than ever before, yet less capable than ever of pursuing self-sustaining growth.

In the Western nations, agricultural development proved to be a key factor in overall economic development. In the era of Western transfer, many governments in Africa, Asia, and Latin America have attempted to bypass agricultural development in their rush to industrialize. They have pursued policies systematically prejudicial to the interests of their rural populations: overtaxing farmers, underpricing their produce, and diverting resources so that the growth of cities and factories may be sustained at a forced pace. Neglect and exploitation have left many poor countries with unnaturally small agricultural sectors in relation to their people's needs or their development potential. Imitating the style of development without capturing its substance, such efforts at development planning have, by and large, succeeded in replicating the structure of the industrialized economies while leaving the populace in poverty.

Some of the resulting distortions may be illustrated by international economic comparisons. (The estimates for poor countries, which come from the World Bank, should not necessarily be treated as reliable or even meaningful, but they are the most commonly used figures in such exercises.) For Peru and Mexico in the early 1980s, the proportion of agriculture in overall GNP was put at roughly 8 percent. This is only half the share that Germany devoted to agriculture in the 1930s, even though Germany then was much more prosperous than Peru or Mexico today by almost any economic measure. By the same token, the share of agriculture in Ecuador's GNP today is apparently smaller than Holland's was in 1950. Bolivia's ratio of agriculture to GNP is lower today than that of Greece, although by any other measure it is Greece that should be considered the more industrialized society. Present-day Nigeria and the Denmark of the early 1950s show roughly equal ratios of agriculture to GNP. Senegal, a nation affected by the Sahelian food crisis, has managed to reduce its current ratio of agriculture to national output down to the level that characterized Japan in the early 1950s. The relation of agriculture to output in Pakistan and India is about the same as in prewar Italy and is only slightly higher in Bangladesh today than it was in Italy at the turn of the century.[17]

The same policies that produce industrialization without prosperity have created an equally paradoxical phenomenon in many less-developed countries: investment without growth. By the estimates of the World Bank, in the early 1960s the ratio of gross domestic investment to GNP in Jamaica, Mauritania, Liberia, and what is now the People's Republic of the Congo was equal to or higher than that of Japan in the early 1950s, at the start of its remarkable boom. Yet over the course of the 1960s and 1970s, while Japan was quadrupling its per capita output, Mauritania and Liberia are said to have raised theirs by less than 40 percent; the People's Republic of the Congo, by the World Bank tally, registered a rise of less than 20 percent; and Jamaica apparently increased its per capita output by a mere 13 percent. It is worth considering the scale of economic mismanagement necessary to achieve such results. We might also wonder how a poor government could maintain such strikingly high rates of capital accumulation in the face of indisputable and continuing economic mismanagement.

Just as agricultural sectors in the third world have been artificially restricted and diminished by national policies, so what is termed investment has been artificially swollen. According to the World Bank, the region of the world with the *lowest* overall investment rate today is the West. In the "middle-income economies," overall rates of gross domestic investment are said to be just short of the historically extraordinary levels Japan achieved at the start of its growth spurt in the 1950s. For the "low-income economies," overall rates of gross domestic investment are higher today than they ever were in the United States or the fastest-growing nations of Western Europe.

But these patterns of investment cannot be taken as a sign of economic promise. In many countries, they have already proved to be manifestly unsustainable—the "debt crisis" affecting so many poor nations is only a formal recognition *in extremis* of this fact. To a distressing degree, the capital buildup to which so many third world governments have committed themselves over the past three decades was guided not by economic logic but by the political imperative of maximizing the resources and power in the hands of the state. The misuse of resources, always costly, is especially hard on the populace of poor societies. It is poor people, after all, who can least easily forgo consumption today, and investment is by definition forgone consumption.

The postwar transfer of resources from Western nations to the less-developed countries, as it has been conducted, appears to have accorded with neither of the two original premises for extending "development assistance": it has not improved the climate for productive international investment, and it has not contributed generally to self-sustaining economic growth. Ironically, financial transfer from the West may actually have made it possible for many nations to avoid participating more fully in the world economy. Under the best of circumstances, financial aid increases the local money supply and thus stimulates inflation and reduces international competitiveness unless offsetting measures are enacted. Many regimes have demonstrated that they are not interested in enacting such measures. After all, overvaluing the local currency makes imports cheap, and to the extent that foreign finance is available, exports are unnecessary.

The justification for "development assistance" that has been voiced increasingly since the early 1970s is the need to "build human capital." There should be no mistaking the crucial importance of human capital in economic growth. Health, education, knowledge, skills, and other immutably human factors determine the maximum pace at which development may proceed. But returns from human capital, as from any other potentially productive resource, depend upon the environment in which they are put to use. Where physical capital is mismanaged and depleted, it would seem unrealistic to expect human capital to be carefully preserved, augmented, and utilized.

Human capital is much more difficult to measure and evaluate than physical capital—a fact that may not have escaped advocates of new spending programs in this area. Nevertheless, it is possible to make some tentative assessments of the effectiveness of some of the human capital programs Western aid has helped sponsor. Consider education. As a very rough rule of thumb, the literacy rate in a poor society today should be similar to its primary school enrollment ratio twenty years earlier. The rule holds in many developing nations but not in all. According to the World Bank, for example, 47 percent of Bangladesh children were enrolled in primary schools in 1960 but the nation's literacy rate in 1980 was only 26 percent. In Togo, the enrollment ratio was 44 percent in 1960, but literacy is put at 18 percent today. In Zaire, the enrollment ratio was 60 percent in 1960, and the literacy rate today may be as low as 15 percent.[18]

Literacy, of course, is notoriously difficult to measure. Such radical discrepancies, however, appear to speak to something more fundamental than inexact definitions. They suggest that spending in the name of human capital can be wasted and often has been. The irony is that such wastage seems most likely to occur as governments restrict their societies' contact with the world economy—preventing them from participating in the learning process that has so demonstrably enhanced the productivity of nations at all economic levels in modern times.

In the final analysis, the economic impact of Western financial transfers on the nations of Asia, Africa, and Latin America seems to depend very largely on the attitudes and inclinations of the recipient government. Taiwan and South Korea were both major beneficiaries of foreign aid in the 1950s and early 1960s, and South Korea has been a major borrower of international capital in the 1970s and the early 1980s. Both countries have used these resources in ways that have enhanced their overall economic productivity, improved their international competitiveness, and increased their ability to take advantage of the growing opportunities afforded by world markets. But easy credit and free aid need not be put to economically constructive purposes. They may also be used for quite different goals—even to underwrite practices so injurious that they could not otherwise be afforded.

America's Role

If opinion surveys are correct, the American people are troubled by our present policies to relieve distress and promote prosperity in the poorer regions of the earth. They are right to be so. As they are currently conducted, American foreign aid policies cannot be relied upon to encourage economic health or self-sustaining growth in low-income nations; indeed, they may actually subsidize practices that perpetuate or even generate poverty in certain places. Such programs betray the wish of the American people to extend their help to the world's least fortunate groups and dangerously compromise America's moral role in the world.

In the decades since they were initiated, the official development policies of the United States have undergone a progressive divorce from their original purposes and principles. To judge by the results of current foreign aid programs, the U.S. government has become comfortable with the idea of conducting a special, separate foreign policy toward the world's poor—a policy whose principles and goals are distinct from, even opposite to, those by which we guide ourselves in the rest of the world. Pursued to their logical conclusion, America's current aid policies would leave poor countries ever less capable of self-sustaining growth and increasingly dependent on foreign largesse to maintain or improve national standards of living. These same aid policies appear to be indifferent to the politically induced suffering that so many poor peoples must endure at the hands of irresponsible or actively mischievous governments. Would we ever think of guiding our relations with another Western people by such rules?

The terrible irony of this situation is that the United States created a new global order at the end of World War II precisely to eliminate the sorts of suffering we now seem to be inadvertently underwriting in different poor countries. The economic pillars of this new order were an International Monetary Fund, a World Bank, and a generalized arrangement for the promotion of international trade; the political framework for this order was to be the United Nations. The liberal international economic system built on those foundations has proved to be the greatest engine of material advance the world has ever known; it has demonstrated its ability to contribute to prosperity in any and all nations willing to avail themselves of its opportunities. The values we impressed upon the original documents of the United Nations not only laid down the guidelines for decent and humane governance but suggested an approach to policy likely to relieve suffering and promote general prosperity. These postwar arrangements, which the United States struggled to produce, have created the greatest opportunities for satisfying the wants and needs of mankind that history has yet seen.

A generation of divisive rhetoric and drift has taken its toll on the United States. What is often easy for Americans to forget is that our divisive rhetoric and drift take an even greater toll on other peoples. The fact is that the United States—as a nation, a power, and an idea—is the greatest hope that the world's poor and unprotected peoples have. It is the American people's unmistakable preference that the peoples of the poorer regions of the earth should eventually be liberated—in the true meaning of that word. The United States can do much to help these peoples in their liberation. But we will not be true to our own preferences, or the promise of our system, if we divorce our policies toward the world's poor from the values, institutions, and international economic arrangements that we cherish for ourselves.

Notes

1. Anders Wijkman and Lloyd Timberlake, *Natural Disasters: Acts of God or Acts of Man?* (Washington, D.C.: Earthscan, 1984), p. 77.

2. *New York Times,* November 24, 1970; and November 27, 1970.

3. *New York Times,* August 30, 1976.

4. *New York Times,* February 27, 1981.

5. Alan Berg, "Famine Contained: Notes and Lessons from the Bihar Experience," *Brookings Institution Reprint Series,* no. 211, 1971.

6. See, for example, Basil Ashton et al., "Famine in China, 1958–61," *Population and Development Review,* vol. 10, no. 4 (December 1984).

7. Emmanuel Urhobo, *Relief Operations in the Nigerian Civil War* (Ibadan: Daystar Press, 1978).

8. Jack Shepherd, *The Politics of Starvation* (New York: Carnegie Endowment for International Peace, 1975).

9. *New York Times,* July 25, 1980; February 15, 1981; March 3, 1984; April 8, 1984.

10. *New York Times,* February 6, 1980; Michael Vickery, *Kampuchea: Politics, Economics, and Society* (London: L. Rienner Publishers, 1986).

11. Much has been written on this. See George Galloway, "The Mengistu Famine," *Spectator,* December 1, 1984; Claude Malhuret, *Mass Deportations in Ethiopia* (Paris: Medicins san Fron-

tières, 1985); Jason W. Clay and Bonnie W. Holcomb, *Politics and the Ethiopian Famine 1984–85* (Cambridge, Mass.: Cultural Survival, 1985); and Arch Puddington, "Ethiopia: The Communist Uses of Famine," *Commentary,* April 1986.

12. Rosanne Klass, "Terror in Afghanistan," *Freedom at Issue,* no. 83 (March–April 1985).

13. Franklin D. Roosevelt, "Address of the President on the Signing of the Agreement Establishing the United Nations Relief and Rehabilitation Administration, November 9, 1943"; reprinted in Samuel I. Rosenman, ed., *The Public Papers and Addresses of Franklin D. Roosevelt, 1943 Volume* (New York: Harper and Row, 1950), p. 504.

14. Organization for Economic Cooperation and Development, *Geographical Distribution of Financial Flows to Developing Nations* (Paris: OECD, 1984). The calculations here are based on this volume and its predecessor series.

15. World Health Organization, "Mortality Trends and Prospects," *WHO Chronicle,* vol. 28 (1974).

16. World Bank, *World Development Report 1982* (New York: Oxford University Press, 1982).

17. Data for developing countries come from various issues of the World Bank's *World Development Report.* Historical figures for Western nations are from Simon S. Kuznets, *Modern Economic Growth* (New Haven, Conn.: Yale University Press, 1966), and Simon S. Kuznets, *The Economic Growth of Nations* (Cambridge, Mass.: Harvard University Press, 1971).

18. *World Development Report,* 1982 and 1983. The World Bank did not publish literacy estimates in the 1984 edition of its report.

THREE
"Human Capital" and Foreign Aid in Africa

In the early days of postwar independence in sub-Saharan Africa, the principal economic rationale offered for the Western aid then being sent to the many new governments just coming to power was the need to "build infrastructure": ports, roads, dams, telecommunications, and the like. Such major, capital-consuming projects, it was then said, would require concessionary foreign sponsorship—for a variety of essentially technical reasons—but they could be expected to be highly productive. Today these former arguments for development aid to the sub-Sahara are less frequently heard. A quarter of a century's experience has attested to pervasive and serious mismanagement of "infrastructure" throughout sub-Saharan Africa; in some cases this infrastructure has been partially or wholly destroyed by the local governments for which it was built.

Advocates of development assistance for sub-Saharan Africa now have a new rationale for aid to the region: the need to build "human capital." By financing programs in health, nutrition, family planning, and education, they now argue, foreign aid can enhance human productivity and thereby promote economic development. In the abstract, this argument may seem unobjectionable. In its proper context— that is, in transferring Western resources to the present governments of sub-Saharan Africa—there is good reason to question whether a human-capital initiative can be generally effective.

Returns from human capital, like returns from physical capital, depend critically upon the environment in which these resources are being put to use. The policies and practices of the overwhelming majority of regimes in sub-Saharan Africa have the predictable effect of radically lowering any anticipated returns from an aid-driven human capital initiative— turning such funds into unproductive social welfare spending, or worse.

The peoples of sub-Saharan Africa live under governments that, with few exceptions, may fairly be described as lawless. The rights to private property, personal liberty, due process, and even to life itself are routinely ignored or violated by the overwhelming majority of sub-Saharan states. Westerners have long complained about the "business environment" in postcolonial Africa: the obligatory graft, the police and army harrassment, the arbitrary restrictions, and the constant threat of summary expropriation. But how much easier is such rule for Westerners—privileged persons with foreign passports—than for ordinary Africans. In Malawi, a country sometimes cited for its comparatively enlightened policies, a device known as the Forfeiture Act permits the government to strip any person suspected of "economic crimes" of all assets and property—permanently—without judicial review or any avenues of appeal.[1] In Mauritania, Western agencies have guessed that as many as 100,000 people in a population of less than 2 million may currently be living in slavery.[2] In several countries, government-instigated atrocities, often tribally motivated, have resulted in hundreds of thousands of civilian deaths. Whatever else may be said of such practices, they do not enhance the productivity of human capital.

If initiatives in health and nutrition were to be effective, a government would ordinarily want demographic and social data for the population in question. Even crude indicators, like mortality rates, can help in identifying the groups in greatest need and in evaluating the effectiveness of programs undertaken on their behalf. It is perhaps significant that the postcolonial states of sub-Saharan Africa have not developed statistical systems capable of providing even such comparatively rudimentary data. The United Nations *Demographic Yearbook* lists seven African states with essentially "complete" death registration systems.[3] Six of these are islands, "African" in the sense that they are nearer to Africa than to any other large land mass. None are in the sub-Sahara. Indeed, in the mid-1970s, a decade and more after independence, many sub-Saharan countries had yet to conduct their first national census. These governments found no compelling reason to count their citizens until the United Nations provided funds for this express purpose.

Western aid agencies—especially the World Bank and the U.S. Agency for International Development—are eager to provide family-planning funds to sub-Saharan Africa in the hope that this may help to lower fertility in the region. In most of these countries, however, local peoples tend to identify *infertility* as their principal population-related concern.[4] In much of Africa the fate of a barren woman is not an enviable one. Even among elites, the preference for large families remains strong.

Many poor Africans seem to fear that family-planning programs will be used to enforce involuntary sterility upon them. These fears are not assuaged by some of the extremist pronouncements on population from the World Bank and AID, by the manifest contempt of local governments for popular concerns, and by the frequency with which the state has been used as a tool of war against tribes not in power.

In March 1986, the *Washington Post* recounted a story of a primary school in rural Kenya from which hundreds of children ran screaming, some scrambling through windows, with the approach of an unfamiliar car: it was thought to contain population workers who would inject them with nonreversible contraceptives.[5] The previous year starving Kenyans in drought-afflicted areas were reported to have refused relief shipments of U.S. corn on the rumor that the corn had been laced with sterilizants.[6] Kenya, of course, is a country in which civil liberties are relatively well secured, and government policies relatively enlightened. It is precisely for those reasons that such stories of deep-seated distrust and fear are noteworthy.

In and of itself, mass literacy is arguably a desirable objective. One should not, however, expect even rapid advances in literacy to bring economic transformation in sub-Saharan Africa under present circumstances. Even if skills and talents are augmented, they will not be put to use in the face of overbearing risks and penalties. (The plight of Tanzania attests to this:

despite its mass literacy campaigns, the country remains mired in poverty, its agriculture shattered by forced collectivization, and its commerce deliberately crippled by a socialist police state.) Moreover, the correspondence between increased expenditures on education and increased literacy cannot be taken for granted.

Statistics from the World Bank's 1986 *World Development Report* illustrate the problem. The report gives breakdowns of central government expenditures for sixteen sub-Saharan countries, excluding South Africa. (That the World Bank apparently can provide such estimates for less than half of the sub-Saharan states in its statistical appendix is revealing in itself.) In the Asian nation of Sri Lanka, where primary education is close to universal, the government spends about $9 per year per person on education. Mali in Africa also devotes about $9 per person per year to education, but its primary school enrollment ratio is said to be only 24 percent. In Senegal, where the figure is put at $18 per person per year, the enrollment ratio is put at 53 percent. Botswana spends nearly ten times as much per person on education as Sri Lanka; yet its primary school enrollment ratio is lower.

This is more than a matter of cost management. Basic strategy is in large part responsible for these results. Throughout sub-Saharan Africa it is college, not grade school, that typically receives priority. Subsidies for the intelligentsia are large. In Sri Lanka, as in most of the West, a year of college costs about five times as much a year as primary school. In Zaire, by contrast, the government spends about forty times as much for a year of college as a year of elementary school; in Nigeria the ratio is over 60 to 1; in Uganda it is over 100 to 1; in Malawi, it is over 200 to 1. In Guinea, where scarcely a third of the country's children are thought to be in grade school, the government was recently spending 30 percent more on college than on primary education.[7] Under such circumstances, it would not seem that the primary constraint on literacy was a simple lack of resources.

There is talk today of "policy reform" in sub-Saharan Africa. According to spokesmen for Western aid agencies, the document produced on June 1, 1986, in the special United Nations General Assembly session on the economic crisis in Africa is testimony to a new attitude on the part of sub-Saharan governments. According to M. Peter McPherson, administrator of AID, "The Africans now realize that fundamentally they have to do some things differently."[8] Yet the very day this UN document was presented to the world media, Kenyan President Daniel arap Moi, in a speech to the nation, "pledged," in the words of the *New York Times,* "to revive flagging attempts to increase Kenyan ownership of private businesses, which are mainly in the hands of Europeans and Asians."[9] These "Europeans" and "Asians" are, in fact, Kenyan citizens, albeit immigrants and ethnic minorities. Lest the racialist intentions of this expensive pledge go unappreciated, Kenya's *Sunday Times* outlined them explicitly: "Everyone appreciates and supports the government's [position] on the issue of Kenyanisation, or better still Africanisation, of business because it is . . . for the betterment of the economical future of this country."[10]

Time and again in postcolonial Africa, governments have displaced merchants and businessmen on the basis of their race, only to lower output, raise costs, and reduce returns for all forms of capital. It is precisely because Kenya is considered one of the more economically responsible states in sub-Saharan Africa that President Moi's announcement and its timing are so significant.

If sub-Saharan states wished to augment human capital, they might begin by attempting to promote civil order and the rule of law—including security of property and person. They might desist from those agricultural and social policies that quite predictably cause nutritional hardship or in extreme cases famine among rural populations. They might manage national finances so as to create stable currencies and reduce restrictions on foreign trade so that their common people might better participate in, and learn from, the greatest educational system of them all: the world economy. None of these suggestions would require external aid.

Western aid today may be compromising economic progress in Africa and retarding its development of human capital. Overseas development assistance (ODA), after all, provides a very substantial fraction of the operating budgets of virtually all governments of sub-Saharan Africa. In 1983, ODA accounted for two-fifths of Liberia's central government budget, for three quarters of Ghana's, and four-fifths of Uganda's.[11] Western aid directly underwrites current policies and practices; indeed, it may actually make possible some of the more injurious policies, which would be impossible to finance without external help.

The public in the United States and other Western countries must face this awful reality honestly and squarely. The West is, at present, directly complicitous with Africa's rulers in the results they inflict upon their subjects. No change in rationales for aid, no new names for programs, no optimistic pronouncements about policy changes in the near future will alter this fact.

Notes

1. U.S. Department of State, *Country Reports on Human Rights Practices for 1986* (Washington, D.C.: 1987), p. 182.

2. John Mercer, *Slavery For Mauritania Today* (Edinburgh: Human Rights Group, 1982).

3. United Nations, *Demographic Yearbook 1983* (New York: United Nations, 1985).

4. See, for example, Odile Frank, "Infertility in Sub-Saharan Africa," *Center For Policy Studies Working Paper #97* (New York: Population Council, 1983).

5. *Washington Post,* March 8, 1986.

6. Ibid.

7. Figures derived from UNESCO, *Statistical Yearbook* (Paris: UNESCO), various issues.

8. *New York Times,* June 1, 1986.

9. Ibid.

10. *Sunday Times* (Nairobi), May 31, 1986.

11. Figures derived from the statistical appendix in World Bank, *World Development Report 1986* (New York: Oxford University Press, 1986).

FOUR

More Myths about Aid to Africa

Over the past few years, the administration, the House, and the Senate have considered economic aid proposals that respond to widespread public concern about the plight and prospects of sub-Saharan Africa's populations. In their analyses of the sub-Saharan region's current problems, views of future solutions to these difficulties, and recommendations for American action, these various proposals have been broadly parallel.

All have been animated by the humanitarian generosity for which the United States is rightly renowned and have reflected the preferences of the American public that the blessings of the twentieth century, including the prosperity that twentieth century knowledge has made possible, be generally available.

Unfortunately, none of these proposals can be expected to advance those objectives effectively. To the contrary, there seems to be good reason to worry whether the funds marshalled in these proposed efforts would not be turned instead to ill-advised or even harmful purposes.

The risk arises because the problems facing local populations seem to be misunderstood. These misunderstandings appear to be most serious, and potentially most consequential, in four areas of current policy: population, environment, debt relief, and policy reform.

Population

Many institutions and individuals involved today in dispensing Western aid to African governments identify population growth as a major obstacle to development in the sub-Sahara and elsewhere. M. Peter McPherson, administrator of the U.S. Agency for International Development (AID), has stated, for example, that "the critical problem of excessive population growth in the Third World . . . constitutes the primary obstacle to increasing per capita food production, reducing malnutrition and chronic disease, and conserving dwindling non-renewable resources."[1] Organizations and individuals of similar view have advocated vigorous population programs for sub-Saharan Africa, to be financed in large part by donations and tax funds from the West.

By and large, this view ignores both the reasons for population growth in Africa today and the likely consequences of aggressive government-sponsored population policies.

As best as can be told, population growth has accelerated rapidly throughout sub-Saharan Africa since the end of the Second World War. It appears that the principal cause of this acceleration has been a pronounced and general drop in the death rate. (In some areas, it appears that fertility may also have increased, but increases in fertility are thought to

102

have been a decidedly secondary factor in the acceleration of population growth for the region as a whole.) Declining death rates, of course, mean that life expectancy is increasing. A pervasive drop in death rates in sub-Saharan Africa, therefore, would indicate a correspondingly pervasive improvement in health conditions over previous levels.[2]

Other things being equal, one would expect improvements in health to be conducive to improvements in productivity. If improvements in health have not led to a general improvement in economic productivity, one must wonder why they have not done so. After all, improvements in health have coincided with improvements in economic productivity, broadly speaking, in both Asia and Latin America in the postwar period.

A fact neglected in much of the discussion of the "population problem" in sub-Saharan Africa is that parents throughout the region appear to prefer large families. The preference is strong, and it is pervasive. It is shared across language groups and spans the income scale; indeed, even Africa's educated elites show an unmistakable preference for large families. Under such circumstances, population programs that seek to reduce parental fertility are likely to be viewed with the deepest suspicion by those who are supposed to benefit most from such programs.

An additional complication arises from the tribal character of contemporary sub-Saharan rule. The overwhelming majority of sub-Saharan countries are composed of collections of tribal groups; typically, governments are dominated by tribes that are in competition with, or hostile toward, other populations within the same territorial boundaries. Postcolonial African history is replete with instances in which government has been used as a tool of tribal war. Under these circumstances, vigorous population programs run the risk of fraying political fabrics even further. How such tensions would contribute to long-term development is not immediately apparent.

American advocates of population programs for sub-Saharan Africa typically insist that they favor voluntary family planning. They typically suggest that they wish parents to be able to attain the family size that parents themselves desire. Their claims are contradicted by the very nature of the programs they are helping to devise.

In most of sub-Saharan Africa, it is *infertility*—not unwanted pregnancies—that women rank as the top priority. The fate of a barren woman in much of the sub-Sahara is a pitiable one. Yet little attention is accorded by Western experts to the "population problem" that most concerns Africans themselves.

If family planning were to be truly voluntary, moreover, population programs would not be linked to numerical population targets, set as objectives for governments to achieve. The groups that promote "voluntary" population programs for sub-Saharan Africa, however, typically see no contradiction in attaching targets of fertility alteration to these programs—even when the explicit goals with regard to fertility alteration are radical and extreme. In Ghana, for example, "voluntary" family planning programs coexist in the government's population program with a target to see national fertility levels reduced by half by the year 2000.[3] How the government might meet such a target voluntarily is by no means clear.

Environmental Degradation

It has often been suggested that a principal cause of sub-Saharan Africa's current economic difficulties is

104

the environment. Many in the aid community have asserted that the region's agricultural—and nutritional—problems have resulted from unusual shortfalls in rain, the progressive extension of the deserts, and deteriorations resulting from population growth.

Such arguments, however, are both misinformed and misleading. There is no "natural" connection between drought and famine in the modern world—even in poor countries. India, for example, suffered serious failures during and after its monsoons for two years in a row in the mid-1960s; the impact on food production was severe, but India did not experience famine as a consequence.[4] Even in a poor society, a government can cope with drought in such a way as to minimize or prevent a rise in death rates—if it is interested in doing so.

Throughout much of the sub-Sahara, erratic rainfall patterns have been a long-standing meteorological condition. The written historical record for most of the sub-Sahara is comparatively recent. As best we know, however, variations in precipitation did not automatically trigger famines in the sub-Sahara in the past—even though localities were typically more isolated, less monetized, and further removed from avenues of outside assistance than they are today. Evidence suggests that local households and communities, then as now, provided for contingency. If these preparations are today in certain areas more likely to be insufficient, one must ask why this would be the case.

The record in Ethiopia under Marxist-Leninist rule may provide a partial answer. In the years since the *Dergue* took power, the country's agricultural system has undergone forced collectivization; its educated and skilled personnel have been terrorized; its relief for the needy, when provided, has been meted out with ethnic and political selectivity. Famine would be the likely eventual result of such practices entirely irrespective of local weather patterns.

Ethiopia is by no means the only state in the sub-Sahara where adverse results of government policy are sometimes ascribed to the weather. In Tanzania, for example, the weather has been officially blamed for regional and countrywide food shortages for more than a decade. Such explanations ignore the economic and human costs of Tanzania's *ujamaa* program of comprehensive, forced agricultural collectivization.

Finally, there has been much talk of the impact of desertification and environmental degradation on sub-Saharan agriculture. These discussions have been largely anecdotal in nature, focusing on particular stories rather than on comprehensive statistics. Such discussions testify to the sorry state of statistical services in the sub-Sahara. Governments that have so much difficulty (and in some cases, so little interest) in counting their own populations are not likely to be able to document changing ecological conditions with either ease or accuracy.

Statistics pertaining to sub-Saharan Africa must be used with caution and care, for they are less reliable than often seems to be assumed. For what it is worth, however, the U.S. Department of Agriculture (USDA) has attempted to assemble estimates of agricultural trends for the various sub-Saharan countries.[5] According to these numbers, there has been considerable variation in performance among countries in the sub-Sahara since the late 1960s. The countries with the worst performance trends over the period from 1969–1971 to 1983–1985, by these estimates, were Angola, Ghana, and Mozambique. None of these countries are in the Sahel—the sub-Saharan region most seriously affected by drought.

According to the USDA's estimates, per capita output of agricultural goods fell by over 40 percent in both Ghana and Mozambique between 1969–1971 and 1983–1985. Over those same years, per capita agricultural output is estimated to have risen in both the Ivory Coast and Malawi. The Ivory Coast shares a long border with Ghana; Malawi is adjacent to, and in fact largely surrounded by, Mozambique. If weather and environment were a decisive factor in the agricultural and economic problems of the sub-Sahara today, one would not expect to witness such strikingly different performance records in neighboring countries.

Preoccupation with the specter of environmental degradation can divert attention from the role of civil order and enlightened government policy in promoting agricultural progress. Political decay, domestic turmoil, and destructive economic or social policies may be expected to affect the ways in which rural populations maintain and enhance the productivity of soil, forests, or pastoral lands. The converse does not obtain.

Preoccupation with environmental degradation, moreover, tends to focus undue attention on agriculture and agricultural production. Although its role is important, agriculture is but a single sector within the economy of even the poorest countries. It is purchasing power that is essential to the well-being of local households, rather than production levels of any single commodity. Increasing local agricultural production often coincides with broad material advance, but it is not indispensable to this process. Between the late 1960s and the mid-1980s, for example, Japan's per capita agricultural output fell by about 10 percent—yet few people would view those as years of economic retrogression in Japan.

Debt Relief

The call for debt relief figures prominently in the aid community's recent proposals for the sub-Sahara. "Rescheduling" the sub-Saharan states' official debt to the U.S. government would involve a partial or full forgiveness of outstanding loans, which in total currently amount to over $2.5 billion. The disbursed and outstanding multilateral and International Monetary Fund (IMF) loans to "low-income Africa" that congressional draft legislation would wish to affect totaled over $16 billion at the end of 1985 by the most recent available published estimate of the World Bank,[6] and would presumably be even greater today.

These amounts, however, pale in comparison with the concessions that have already been requested in international forums—proposals, it should be noted, about which administration officials have to date made only favorable general comments. The UN Programme of Action for African Recovery and Development 1986–1990, adopted unanimously by the UN General Assembly in June 1986, would require, in the estimate of the Organization for African Unity, the forgiveness of *$35–55 billion* in outstanding international debts to sub-Saharan states.[7]

The idea that debt relief would stimulate material advance in the sub-Sahara arises from a number of seriously mistaken impressions. It is a mistake, for example, to assume that the governments in question "simply can't pay back" the money they have borrowed—much less make good on the other obligations to which they have committed themselves in contract. In most countries in the sub-Sahara, key industries have been nationalized in the postcolonial period, and government-owned enterprises now figure prominently in the economy. Most of these governments have other assets as well.

It is a mistake, moreover, to assume that the actions that might facilitate the redemption of these obligations would necessarily prejudice prospects for material advance or endanger the poorest populations of the countries in question. To the contrary, the policy changes that would enable sub-Saharan states to repay their debts more easily are consistent with renewed economic growth and improved popular welfare—including improved welfare for the poorest fractions of these local populations.

The "debt crisis" now afflicting sub-Saharan Africa is, to a very significant degree, a crisis of productivity. Repayment problems have typically arisen because the borrowing states have not earned with the foreign capital at their disposal sums sufficient to meet the original—and often extremely forbearing—interest and amortization schedules for their loans. The same policies that led to low rates of return on borrowed foreign capital also depressed exports, discouraged cost management in public and private enterprises, and restricted the economic opportunities of the less-privileged ethnic groups and social strata.

It is a mistake to think that forgiving official loans from the West to the governments of the sub-Sahara will necessarily, unambiguously, or even generally reduce the prospective burdens and privations for Africa's subject populations in the years to come. As has been noted, much of the lending to low-income Africa in the postwar period has been arranged on extremely easy terms. In 1985 (the latest year for which the World Bank has provided comprehensive estimates) over \$35 billion of official loans from Western governments and multilateral organizations were disbursed and outstanding to the governments of low-income Africa.[8] This sum was estimated to account for over four-fifths of all international loans to these countries. Since almost all official loans to the sub-Sahara are arranged on terms more favorable than could be negotiated in the commercial marketplace, this means that about four-fifths of the international borrowings of low-income Africa are concessional in nature.

If concessional lending involves an element of charity, it correspondingly reduces the rate of return that must be earned on borrowed money in order to pay it back. In Africa's current circumstances, we must ask whether it is a kindness to the local populations of the sub-Sahara to hold their rulers to a lower standard of economic performance than the one that commercial borrowers must expect to maintain if they are to attract and repay foreign capital. It is, after all, not the populations of the sub-Sahara who have been granted concessional loans from the West: such lending has, to the contrary, been awarded to their rulers.

The terms upon which a state may secure funding can go far in shaping its own expectations and conduct. Needless to say, most governments in the sub-Sahara, in their present straits, do not need to be encouraged to be less thrifty or less accountable or to confuse more thoroughly the concepts of commerce and charity. Yet this is precisely what the extension of concessional lending to the sub-Sahara has served to do.

Debt relief would vastly intensify this problem.

To enforce a further debt relief on official loans is necessarily to reduce the rate of return that is expected on those particular funds borrowed by those particular states. Already the real rate of interest on much of the official lending to the sub-Sahara is zero or negative. To drive down the real rate of interest on those loans still further will have the effect of excusing local policies that have been positively destructive in their economic consequence.

Retroactively excusing the rulers of the sub-Sahara from their international obligations would not seem to be the most promising strategy by which to encourage governmental accountability and responsibility in low-income Africa. Nor would such a signal be expected to bolster civic virtue—a quality already in extremely scarce supply in much of the sub-Sahara. To the contrary, lawfulness in the sub-Saharan Africa may be expected to suffer directly as a consequence of any general debt relief program advanced, or endorsed, by Western countries. The primary victims of such a policy, in the event, will not be Western taxpayers but rather the very groups and individuals that their funds are meant to help.

Policy Reform

Proponents of extra aid to the sub-Sahara are today virtually unanimous in recommending that American funds be used to promote "economic policy reform." The idea is that self-sustaining economic development can be fostered by paying governments to adopt policies believed to be conducive to this general purpose.

The concept of aid for economic policy reform is no longer new. It represents the current orthodoxy among official institutions dispensing development aid to governments in Asia, Africa, and Latin America. AID has for a number of years identified policy reform as one of the four principal overseas objectives to be secured by its spending. By the same token, the World Bank has for the better part of a decade awarded "structural adjustment" loans to recipient states; such loans, which constitute an increasing fraction of World Bank lending, are not attached to any specific project (as the bank's Articles of Agreement require every loan to be), but instead are expected to underwrite changes in government policy. The UN Programme of Action explains much of its request for external aid in terms of the need to support policy reform in the sub-Sahara.

Indeed, some American enthusiasts have already come to believe that public money is no longer enough to encourage policy reform. In October 1985, in a now famous speech, U.S. Treasury Secretary James Baker suggested that American banks lend an additional $20 billion to specific debtor governments, above and beyond the level these banks took to be commercially prudent. The rationale for attempting to direct additional private capital into states to which the proposed creditors thought it ought not go, Baker explained, was that these funds might help the states in question undertake "policy reforms" that would eventually make them creditworthy.

In the abstract, few observers would oppose the prospect of policy reform or economic policy reform in sub-Saharan Africa—far from it. To the extent that sub-Saharan Africa's current circumstances are the result of the practices and actions of local governments, corrective steps by these states would be not only economically beneficial but absolutely necessary to enhance prospects for material advance.

Unfortunately, there is no reason to expect foreign aid programs financed under the rubric of "policy reform" to be capable of bringing about these corrective steps or even of supporting corrective adjustments in any general fashion.

The policy reform programs for less-developed countries that are currently so popular with, and so heavily subsidized by, agencies dispensing public development aid from the West neglect a simple but rather important fact. The actions of a government depend upon the intentions of the rulers. Providing a government with additional, windfall resources will increase its freedom to maneuver. This will make it easier for the group or groups in power to pursue their own objectives, whatever these may be. Additional resources will not, in themselves, alter the intentions of the group or groups in power.

By and large, the intentions of governments are altered most effectively by altering the group in power. Since few regimes view their own liquidation with equanimity, proponents of policy reform programs face a dilemma. If a government voluntarily accepts aid for policy reform, this will likely mean that the group or groups in power have come to the conclusion that the program would not interfere with the pursuit of the regime's own intentions. If, however, a program of policy reform promises significantly to constrain, compromise, or alter the ability of the regime to pursue its ambitions and if the acceptance of such aid is the prerogative of the state in question, such a policy reform package will likely be refused by the group or groups in power—and may well be decried as an attempt to interfere in domestic affairs or to impinge upon national sovereignty.

Providing a government with the aid to pursue its own intentions more effectively need not conduce to either material advance or the well-being of the local population. This has been demonstrated on more than one occasion in postcolonial Africa. We may recall Tanzania's ill-fated *ujamaa* program. That program, which involved the forced collectivization of so much of the country's rural population and did so much to shatter the country's agricultural economy, was financed in large part by overseas development aid, particularly aid from the World Bank. Surveying these Tanzanian results in the late 1970s, W. David Hopper, then and now a vice president of the bank, wrote that "as long as food aid . . . is supplied to Tanzania by the industrial countries, the social experiment (i.e., *ujamaa*) will continue."[9] One may wonder not only about the continuance of *ujamaa*, but about its initiation; would a program so manifestly destructive in its economic consequence have been undertaken in the first place without ensured sources of overseas aid from which to continue to finance the operation of the state?

Not all sub-Saharan governments, of course, have demonstrated the contempt for their subjects and indifference to economic result that have been articulated so clearly over the years by the rulers of Tanzania. At the same time, the constellation of intentions represented in the many governments of the sub-Saharan can, in total, hardly be described as an auspicious point of departure. Liberty, integrity of person, security of property, rule of law—these exist in a handful of places in the sub-Sahara. What should we expect from programs that will empower current governments to pursue more effectively their ambitions and objectives?

Even with aid that is tied to a given project, the intentions and capabilities of the recipient government are of enormous importance. "Project aid," however, is supposed to result in a tangible product—the project itself. A given project—a road, a dam, an agricultural research station—may be shown to have been a failure. By contrast, no program of policy reform can ever be demonstrated to have failed. If original targets and objectives of "reform" are not achieved, it may always be argued that unforeseeable events were to blame: that the project itself was a success and that things would have been even worse without it.

AID's record of achieving the initial objectives of its policy reform programs has to date been extremely unpromising. It is no secret that, since at least the early 1970s, AID has been explicitly concerned ever more with relief work and social welfare, ever less with the particulars of fostering conditions conducive to "self-sustaining economic development." This is a trend that has been actively and purposefully encouraged by Congress.

Yet the fact is that development agencies and public financial institutions with more freedom to maneuver have not fared much better than AID in their attempts to enforce policy reform on the "partners" receiving their aid. The World Bank's structural adjustment initiative has been described as innovative and successful and not only by World Bank personnel themselves. With the possible exception of Turkey, however, I am not aware of a single instance in which a country awarded "structural adjustment" funds has subsequently been judged more creditworthy, or more attractive to investment, by the international financial community. Even in Turkey, subsequent events were decisively influenced by a military coup that overturned the government with which the policy reform program had been negotiated. As for the International Monetary Fund, a number of studies by European and American economists have suggested that recipients of its "short-term" assistance are quite likely to be return candidates for further "temporary" aid.[10] While the IMF has a reputation for imposing strict conditions with its loans, results suggest that its actual ability (or inclination) to enforce "conditionality" may be limited. Whereas for example IMF loans are typically extended to help local governments achieve "stabilization" of their economies, such loans have frequently been followed by a prolonged period of rapid or even accelerating domestic inflation—precisely the opposite of what stabilization is commonly understood to entail.

There is at least one avenue of policy reform that proponents of policy reform aid programs often neglect to consider. It is called the international marketplace. The international marketplace has at its disposal considerable amounts of lendable capital. It is also quite flexible, being capable of extending capital to borrowing countries through quite a variety of different programs. The international marketplace is constantly testing and assessing the "policy environment" of the countries of Asia, Africa, and Latin America. If the local environment is deemed to be auspicious, funds will be available, both to private concerns and to local governments. If the policy environment is deemed to be inauspicious, new funds will no longer be available, or will be available only at a premium—or will be available only after the international marketplace is satisfied that effective corrective steps are actually in progress (not simply promised).

In the international marketplace, unlike development aid agencies, the review process takes place daily. It occurs spontaneously and relies on an information system more complex and far-reaching than any development official might attempt deliberately to construct. This version of conditionality, moreover, often actually does cut the supply of international funds to governments when these governments violate the letter or the spirit of their international agreements and obligations. Note that this avenue of policy reform does not presuppose ongoing subsidization by Western taxpayers.

No marketplace, of course, operates with perfect efficiency. If it did, there could be no role for, or purpose to, entrepreneurship. And insofar as they articulate human choices, markets may also articulate errors in judgment. Yet it is one thing to recognize these realities and quite another to improve upon them.

The burden of proof is on the proponents of policy reform programs. They must be able to argue that their interventions will be more conducive to policy reform than nothing at all—that is to say, than simply allowing the international marketplace to enforce policy reform on states that would, without development aid, be obliged to establish creditworthiness by actions and conduct consonant with attracting capital. Moreover, proponents of policy reform aid programs should be prepared to argue that the reforms they propose to purchase from local governments would constitute so dramatic an improvement over the ordinary workings of the international marketplace as to justify the taxation of Western populations to underwrite the process.

Conclusion

In criticizing specific initiatives being implemented in, or considered for, sub-Saharan Africa, I do not mean that there is little to be done to improve the economic prospects for the region. Exactly the opposite is true.

Greater governmental interest in civil order and respect for property—including the property of their own subjects—could be expected to have a predictable and positive impact not only on the ability of the sub-Saharan states to repay their debts but also on the well-being of local subject populations. Pursuit of more liberal trade regimes and domestic policies would perhaps increase the capacity to generate not only export revenues but also domestic output, demand for labor, and, ultimately, purchasing power for the poor.

The World Bank's *World Development Report 1987* gives figures on the breakdown in recent years of central government expenditures for fourteen sub-Saharan states, excluding South Africa. (That the bank can provide such figures for less than half of the thirty-three sub-Saharan states in its statistical appendix is revealing in itself—perhaps especially in what it portends for ongoing and proposed policy reform programs.) For the thirteen sub-Saharan states for which both recent government expenditure breakdowns and per capita GNP estimates are printed, the unweighted average of overseas development assistance to central government expenditure was close to 40 percent. For the group as a whole, disbursements of overseas development assistance were the single largest source of central government current revenue; in nine of the twelve countries for which figures permitted comparison, receipts from overseas development assistance exceeded the combined total of revenues raised from income taxes, corporate profit taxes, and captial gains taxes.

Thus, to a very great degree, Western aid, including American aid, directly underwrites current policies and practices in the sub-Sahara. Indeed, it may make possible some of the more injurious policies that would be impossible to finance without external help. It might be well to consider the moral and practical consequences of this arrangement before underwriting it on an even greater scale.

Notes

1. *Department of State Bulletin,* vol. 83 (May 1983), p. 53.

2. Population figures for sub-Saharan Africa are very much less accurate and comprehensive than some commentators seem to suppose. There is, for example, not a single country in the sub-Sahara with a near-complete registration system for either births or deaths. See United Nations, *Demographic Yearbook 1985* (New York: United Nations, 1987).

3. World Bank, *World Development Report 1984* (New York: Oxford University Press, 1984), p. 159.

4. Alan Berg, "Famine Contained: Notes and Lessons from the Bihar Experience," *Brookings Institution Reprint Series,* no. 211, 1971.

5. U.S. Department of Agriculture, Economic Research Service, *World Indices of Agricultural and Food Production* (Washington, D.C.), various issues.

6. Derived from World Bank, *World Debt Tables: 1986/87 Edition* (Washington, D.C.: World Bank, 1987).

7. Since this total could far exceed the total of disbursed and outstanding debt for "low-income Africa" to Western governments and multilateral development banks, it would seem to

envision a substantial "rescheduling" of African states' debts to private lenders as well.

8. Derived from *World Debt Tables*.

9. W. David Hopper, "Distortions of Agricultural Development Resulting from Governmental Prohibitions," in T. W. Schultz, ed., *Distortions of Agricultural Incentives* (Bloomington, Ind.: Indiana University Press, 1978), p. 76.

10. See, for example, Roland Vaubel, "The Moral Hazard of IMF Lending," *The World Economy,* vol. 6, no. 3 (September 1983); and Jeffrey D. Sachs, "Managing the LDC Debt Crisis," *Brookings Papers on Economic Activity,* 2:1986.

FIVE

Democracy and the "Debt Crisis" in Latin America: A Comment

This chapter was originally prepared as a comment on a paper delivered in August 1985 at Airlie House in Warrenton, Virginia, by Professor Hugo Assmann, a prominent Brazilian exponent of "liberation theology." Professor Assmann's topic was the improvement of democracy in Latin America and the debt crisis. His presentation included the following points.

First, the ordinary workings of the contemporary international economic order, which Professor Assmann termed "capitalist," were said to inflict extraordinary violence and suffering upon the common people of Africa, Asia, and particularly Latin America. He asserted that the "capitalist" international order enforced a sort of "genocide" upon the world's poor and stated that this system exacted an annual toll of 40 million unnecessary deaths on the "third world."

Second, Professor Assmann argued that the plight of ordinary people in Latin America (and possibly the entire third world) was being worsened further still by Western countries' harsh and aggressive policies toward government borrowing in low-income areas. A variety of circumstances, he argued, had made it impossible as a practical matter for many governments to repay international debts owed in the mid-1980s. Attempting to make good on these debts, he continued, would only wreak still further destruction in the lives of the common people in the countries concerned and might indeed threaten their very survival. Nevertheless, banks and governments in Western countries were pressing for a full payment of interest, principal, and arrearages—even, Professor Assmann wryly noted, as governments in developed countries were erecting trade barriers that would prevent the very exports that might earn Latin American countries the necessary funds.

Third, Professor Assmann charged that the Western posture on debt repayment was endangering "democratization" in Latin America. In the early 1980s, he said, many Latin governments previously ruled by military juntas or other varieties of autocrats were in the process of returning to popular representation. If Westerners continued to press their debt claims, he warned, Latin American governments might be forced to take measures so unpopular, and so injurious to local populations, that democratic currents in their countries would be unable to withstand the reaction.

Professor Assmann noted that Fidel Castro had declared Latin America's debts to the Western world to have been unjustly contracted and that the Cuban ruler had urged debtor countries to repudiate them. Professor Assmann suggested that a less "confrontational" approach to the debt problem would be preferable. He urged North Americans negotiating over the debt to take into account the welfare of the poor and voiceless masses in Latin America, for "the necessary negotiations to resolve the debt crisis have a lot to do with threatened lives."

There is an issue on which I find myself in total agreement with Professor Assmann: protectionism. Protectionist trade policies, and other actions that unnaturally restict commercial and financial contacts between rich and poor countries, create needless economic hardships. Such protectionism reduces the opportunities for income generation in less-developed nations, thus affecting earnings, output, employment, and economic efficiency. At the same time, barriers against entry and competition in the domestic markets of the more affluent nations punish consumers in those countries by reducing diversity of selection and supporting unnecessarily high prices. Higher prices in turn mean higher costs of production, reduced competitiveness, constricted output, and unnecessarily low employment. The protectionist measures adopted by developed nations have an additional, and ironic, effect of making it more difficult for less-developed nations to earn the foreign currency they need to make good on their sizable debts to private and public institutions in the West. (Of course, the adverse consequences of protectionism arise regardless of whether the state imposing it is "developed" or "developing"; the array of protectionist devices employed by indebted and comparatively poor nations to prevent competition in their local markets is far-reaching, and their impact is consequential.)

Apart from protectionism, I disagree with Professor Assmann over all the substantive areas touched upon in his discourse. Although the differences that separate us may center upon our contrasting philosophical perspectives, they include interpretations of fact and even issues of fact themselves.

Professor Assmann seems to cast Fidel Castro in the role of "tough cop" in the current confrontation over external debt in Latin America. Thus, any government or actor adopting a posture even fractionally less hostile to Western creditor institutions than Castro's own are cast as "nice cops." Such actors can then be described as "moderate" or "pragmatic," not by the merits of their argruments but by their location on a spectrum of negotiating stances artificially extended by the inclusion of Castro's proposals within the realm of serious discussion.

There is little reason to grant Fidel Castro either attention or authority on the questions of economic independence or financial self-reliance. Castro's Cuba is a more dependent country today than when he came to power.

Economically, Cuba is scarcely less a one-crop economy today than it was before its "liberation." According to Lord Thomas, the well-known student of Cuban history, "in the forty years before Batista's final overthrow, sugar accounted for 82% of Cuban exports."[1] Figures are less certain for Cuba today; it is difficult, after all, to measure real trade and output in a country where prices reflect imposed governmental preferences rather than scarcity or articulated demand. According to Cuba's official *Statistical Yearbook*, however, export revenues from the sugar harvest accounted for 83 percent of Cuba's total export earnings in 1980.[2] So much for "diversification."

But even the totality of Cuba's exports is insufficient to pay for everything that the Cuban government must now import to continue its existence. Cuba today relies upon large and steady subsidies from the USSR simply to function. The size of these annual contributions should give pause to any advocate of "economic independence." Again, the precise magnitude of economic flows is difficult to determine when the prices of goods and services are set at the command of a regime. But there is little doubt that gifts and loans from the COMECON bloc finance about a third of Cuba's current economic consumption.[3] Put another way, direct donations and lines of credit advanced by other Communist nations allow contemporary Cuba to live on half again as much as it could if it had to purchase everything it consumes today on the basis of its own production.

No other country in this hemisphere is so heavily dependent on foreign largesse. Nor is any other nation in this hemisphere so beholden to its creditors. The Soviet Union is neither forbearing nor shy toward those regimes under its financial obligation. And Cuba's ruble indebtedness, now mounting by several billion each year, is a lever that Moscow does not hesitate to use. We can recall the spectacle of Fidel Castro, self-proclaimed exponent of nonalignment and national independence, warmly endorsing the Soviet invasion of Czechoslovakia shortly after Soviet energy supplies to his island were "accidentally" interrupted.[4] Today, Cuba depends even more on the Soviet economic system than it did in 1968—and what is required of Cuba in return is commensurately greater. Tens of thousands of Cubans have been sent to the labor-scarce regions of Eastern Europe and the USSR as a sort of human amortization on the Cuban national debt.[5] They toil at artificially reduced wages so that their government can make a partial payment to its Warsaw Pact allies on the enormous financial debt it owes them. But Cuba's effort to redeem its government debt through traffic in its own citizens is not limited to *bracero* socialism. Today Cuban soldiers are dying in Angola, Ethiopia, Mozambique, and Afghanistan; this, too, is a *direct* response to their government's enormous ruble obligations. If Professor Assmann wishes to find a vivid illustration of the violence forced upon a local population by international indebtedness, he need search no farther.

But this is not the violence Professor Assmann sees. He argues instead that the international system of commercial finance and trade in which Western nations play so great a part is wreaking extraordinary destruction in the less-developed countries. As he portrays the arrangement, it is actually murderous. By his account, the current international system can be connected with what he says are 40 million needless, even unnatural, deaths in the third world every year.

It is necessary to inject some facts into this discussion. There is a considerable literature on world population trends. Demographic estimates pertaining to less-developed countries are generally least reliable for precisely those areas where poverty is greatest and mortality is highest. As a best guess, however, the number of deaths for the entirety of the human race currently comes to somewhere around 50 million a year. (The World Bank's 1985 *World Development Report,* whose figures generally reflect the received wisdom in the development business, would place the total number of deaths in the world in 1983 at 48.3 million, although the margins of error suggested by such a precise estimate—to the tenths of millions—are obviously unwarranted.)

Let us say, for the sake of argument, that the

actual number of deaths is higher—say, a global total of 60 million a year. To say that 40 million of these deaths are unnecessary would be to say that at least two-thirds of the people in the world who die each year should not do so.

The point at issue here is not ethics, but arithmetic. To presume that upwards of two-thirds of the deaths in the world each year are unnecessary is, in effect, to posit a "natural" lifespan for human beings of 120 years, or even greater. It would be impossible to reduce the annual toll of death on earth by 40 million without raising the current expectation of life at birth for the planet as a whole to at least 120 years. While a life expectancy at birth of this order, and the good health that would presumably accompany it, may be desired by many national populations, these are within the grasp of none. The healthiest nation of the earth is now Japan; its life expectancy falls short of this target by more than 40 years. It serves neither practical not ethical purposes to treat the ethereal desideratum of a 120-year lifespan as a feasible norm.

For what it is worth, the *World Development Report 1985* places the total number of deaths for Africa, Latin America and the Caribbean, and Asia (minus Japan and the USSR) at under 39 million. Under such conditions, reducing the annual toll of deaths in these regions by 40 million would be an imposing task.

A nation's life expectancy is an important indicator of a population's well-being. As best we know, the gap in life expectancy between the United States and Canada and the rest of the hemisphere, taken as a whole, is now close to a decade. This gap speaks to meaningful and important differences in a variety of life chances. It is well to remember, however, that the gap in lifespans between North America and Latin

FOREIGN AID AND AMERICAN PURPOSE

America was much larger in the recent past. For the early 1950s, for example, the difference in life expectancy between the two regions has been estimated at about *two* decades.[6] Thus, this most significant of material inequalities has been narrowing, not widening, and it narrowed substantially in recent decades. And the narrowing is not just a trick of averages. The data that I have had a chance to review indicate that overall levels of life expectancy in every Latin American society with reliable statistics have been increasing over recent decades.

No data suggest that national life expectancy has fallen *anywhere* in Latin America in the years since the onset of the so-called "financial crisis." In Argentina, where such data may be regarded as reasonably reliable, infant mortality is down. This is also true in Venezuela. In Chile infant mortality dropped sharply in the early 1980s. We can be less confident about Mexico, since death registration there is incomplete, but the tentative indications are that infant mortality has dropped, not risen, in the period since September 1982. Although infant mortality figures for Brazil are somewhat conjectural, owing to incomplete registration of both births and deaths, no statistical evidence suggests that the nation's slow but steady improvements in overall health have been arrested or reversed. In short, if the argument that current international economic arrangements are contributing to the "murder" of great numbers of people in Latin America is to be treated as a verifiable proposition, it appears to be demonstrably false.

There has been much discussion of the causes of Latin America's current debt problems. One school of thought, which might be called "structuralist," seeks explanations for the current problem of Latin Amer-

128

ica's nonperforming loans in the relative size of various sectors of these economies. Such talk fastens upon, for example, the ratio of external debt to GNP or the ratio of service payments to export earnings. While these comparisons can highlight economic trends, they do not speak to the fundamental causes of financial difficulties. A more fruitful way to pursue the issue is to consider the rate of return being earned by borrowed money in comparison with the rate of interest that must be paid back on it.

Not all third world countries with substantial international financial obligations now find themselves in financial difficulty. The example of South Korea immediately comes to mind. Korea's foreign debt today approaches $50 billion; yet it seems to meet its payments of interest and principal on time and has not found it necessary to enter into "rescheduling" negotiations. Why is this? The answer is that, to date, the government has managed to earn a higher rate of return on the foreign money it is putting to use than it is obliged to pay back in interest.

To my way of thinking, any discussion of a debt crisis in Latin America raises the question of how those funds were spent. What is the cause of what must obviously have been low rates of return on the enormous quantity of money borrowed? Understanding Latin America's current difficulties requires us to address this question directly and honestly.

Some claim that vast amounts of money have been lost to theft and corruption in Latin America over the past decade. I am not in a position to judge the accuracy of those claims. It is my inclination, however, to suspect that theft and corruption are not the main explanation for Latin America's current financial difficulties. From an arithmetic standpoint, the case does not look plausible. Simply put, it would be difficult for any person or group to steal the sum of money required to drive rates of return on borrowed funds down to the level that was reached by some of Latin America's debtor nations.

The explanation for these low rates of return, it seems to me, is largely to be found in a systematically unproductive application of public funds. Faced with easy access to credit from Western banks in the wake of the OPEC oil price increases, many governments seem to have adjusted their policies toward less, rather than more, productive uses of capital. This seems not solely to have been a question of pursuing ill-advised or mismanaged investment programs on the public account. In many nations much of the borrowed money appears to have been used to maintain unsustainably high levels of consumption for the general population through a complex and ambitious array of subsidies.[7] Common rhetoric notwithstanding, these subsidies conferred immediate benefit on very broad portions of the populations in question. Indeed, their broad incidence was precisely the reason for their widespread popularity.

A chorus of voices is raised to insist that Latin America's debts to Western institutions are too large to repay. Professor Assmann seems to concur with these voices. His paper and his talk assert that it is quite impossible to make good on these debts.

If this point is pursued as a proposition in arithmetic, rather than ideology, it is not convincing. In most of the Latin American nations where the "rescheduling" of debts is under way, the public sector owns 40, 50, or even 60 percent of the country's industrial base. It is highly illogical to state, on the one hand, that a government owns half or more of a country's industrial base and to say, on the other, that it has no assets that might be sold to help repay its various international obligations. Many Latin American governments, not just Brazil and Argentina, also possess large tracts of public land that could also be sold if there were a serious intention to make good on contracted debts. I have not, to date, heard any discussion of such measures. There is a distinction between inability and unwillingness to pay a debt, and it must not be obscured.

Indeed, the policy changes that would enable Latin American nations to pay their debts more easily are not inconsistent with improved welfare of the masses, particularly of the poorest fractions of those populations—far from it. The same policies that led to low rates of return on foreign debt also depressed exports, discouraged cost management in private and public enterprises, and restricted the opportunities of the less-privileged segments of society for increased earnings and employment. Pursuit of more liberal trade regimens and domestic policies would perhaps increase the capability to generate not only export revenues but also domestic output, demand for labor, and, ultimately, purchasing power for the poor.

Professor Assmann suggests that pressing the debt issue will jeopardize the prospects for democratization in Latin America. My own perspective is quite different. It seems to me that assuming full responsibility for the debt would *promote* democratization, not endanger it.

Two things that separate democracies from dictatorships are responsibility and liberty, secured by law. To qualify or reject one's obligation to repay contracted debts is necessarily to raise serious questions about both responsibilities and individual rights.

FOREIGN AID AND AMERICAN PURPOSE

Western nations, it is sometimes said, are dangerously strong. Western banks are often accused of having unfair bargaining power in their negotiations with debtor nations. Let us take such rhetoric at its face value. If the rights of the strong can be summarily repealed and dismissed, what does this portend for the weak? If a government willingly reneges on its obligations to other sovereign states, what does this suggest about its attitude toward those individuals who live under its administration? If law can be interpreted to allow violation of the rights of the influential at the pleasure of the state, what protections can the poor and defenseless expect? The poor and the weak are always more vulnerable to the abuse of power than the privileged. To deny protection or absolve responsibility for one segment of society is a perilous business, for it exposes all to risk. Thus, repudiating the debt would seem to lead Latin American nations away from true democracy, not toward it.

Notes

1. Hugh Thomas, *Cuba: The Pursuit of Freedom* (New York: Harper & Row, 1971), p. 1152.

2. *Anuario Estadistico de Cuba 1985* (Havana: Comite Estatal de Estadisticas, n.d.).

3. According to the British Foreign Ministry, for example, the East Bloc subsidy to Cuba exceeded $5 billion US in 1985. See United Kingdom, Foreign and Commonwealth Office, *Soviet Bloc Aid to "Special Friends"* (London: Ministry of Foreign Affairs, August 1987). For an earlier treatment of the issue, see Nick Eberstadt and Thomas E. Ricks, "The Cost of Pax Sovietica," *The New Republic,* December 31, 1981.

4. This is discussed, among other places, in Carmelo Mesa-Lago, *The Economy of Socialist Cuba: A Two Decade Perspective* (Albuquerque: University of New Mexico Press, 1981).

5. See, for example, the Cuban paper *Granma,* December 16, 1986. Moscow has recently announced that as many as 80,000 Cubans will be working by 1995 "near Khabarovsk" alone. (Foreign Broadcast Information Service, USSR–International Affairs, May 18, 1987.) These workers will apparently be assigned to lumber camps in the Soviet Far East. One may recall that this same work was assigned a few decades earlier to Soviet prisoners in the death camps within Stalin's Gulag.

6. United Nations, *Demographic Indicators of Countries: Estimates and Projections as Assessed in 1980* (New York: United Nations, Department of International Economic and Social Affairs, 1982).

7. On this score, see Jeffrey D. Sachs, "External Debt and Macroeconomic Performance in Latin America and East Asia," *Brookings Papers on Economic Activity,* 2:1985.

SIX

Recommendations for Restoring Purpose to American Foreign Aid in the 1980s

American foreign aid policies must be made more effective. Their effectiveness cannot be increased, however, without an appreciation of the larger purposes to which they are to be applied. In principle, these purposes are clear. The first is to augment American political power throughout the world. The second is to support the postwar liberal international economic order that the United States helped create and is committed to preserving.

These purposes are closely related. With its particular political values, the United States can achieve greatest security under a world order that accepts as legitimate the free international flow of information,

The author would like to thank Gifford Combs and Clifford Lewis for many hours of enlightening discussions on some of the topics addressed in this chapter.

135

trade, technology, and capital; that does not question the right of people to act to improve their material well-being; and that embraces the rule of law and the propriety of enlightened governance. Conversely, the use of American power to protect a system that offers all nations and peoples opportunity—unmatched by alternative arrangements—to participate in broad-based material advance is not only a strategic goal but an objective dictated by U.S. moral and humanitarian concerns. The liberal international economic order America helped create remains the best broad hope for the world's poor and disadvantaged peoples. The United States should use its power—military, financial, moral—to protect it.

Just as the wedding of moral purpose and international power is fundamental to Americans' view of their own nation, so too should it govern the country's approach to foreign aid. In a consideration of foreign assistance, however, it is best to distinguish three separate concerns.

Humanitarian Aid

As current events in Ethiopia demonstrate, much of mankind is still stalked by the prospect of famine and sudden, unexpected, life-threatening disasters. Both private voluntary organizations and the American governmental relief apparatus have developed impressive expertise in saving lives in such emergencies. These efforts have demonstrated that it is possible to prevent abnormal rises in death rates so long as donors receive early warning of the impending crisis and the government of the territory in question does not obstruct rescue efforts.

The American people have consistently proved

that their compassion for those in distress abroad is mitigated neither by the ideology of the government of the stricken territory nor the relationship of that government with the United States. In the early 1920s, for example, private donations funded Herbert Hoover's American Relief Administration as it worked in Soviet Russia to save, according to George Kennan, the lives of "several million children, who would otherwise have died."[1] Americans are donating millions of dollars to support relief operations in Marxist-Leninist Ethiopia; these contributions mounted spontaneously after information on the famine was released. Ethiopia's ruling *Dergue,* like the Soviet Politburo, is systematically hostile to American purposes in the world, but this fact did not constrain Americans' charitable impulse. Americans' commitment to humanitarian relief is moral, not political, in derivation. It represents a basic commitment from one people to another and is based on the belief that the sanctity of life creates a transcendent obligation to act to save others.

American policies toward humanitarian aid should better reflect these beliefs. Doing so will require changes in the posture and the actions of the U.S. government. The official American response to the disasters of imperiled peoples should not be compromised by the hesitation and political calculation that, by some news accounts, affected the early U.S. efforts in the current Ethiopian crisis. There should be no doubt on the part of U.S. governmental agencies that Americans feel it is unseemly to submit endangered populations to trial by *realpolitik.*

Washington should make a more encompassing and articulate commitment to help populations imperiled by famines and other temporary emergencies.

In a broad sense, such a policy should commit the United States unreservedly to the rescue of those whose lives are threatened by emergencies and disasters—irrespective of their government's attitude toward the United States or "human rights" or any other consideration. The only condition that Washington should place on such aid is that local governments not obstruct the efforts of outside agencies to act in the afflicted areas. This broad commitment to famine and emergency relief might help save millions of lives in stricken regions that otherwise would be lost in future years. It will also be obvious that great loss of life from famine and disaster would occur only under governments that refused to let America make good on its humanitarian commitment to the people of the world.

Expanded humanitarian commitment would require several important changes in current government relief policies:

• *Upgrade substantially the priority accorded emergency relief within U.S. foreign aid policy.* At present, only about 1 percent of the total foreign aid budget is allocated to emergency assistance. Even with the Food for Peace or P.L. 480 Program, less than a sixth of program resources in recent years have been earmarked for famines, emergencies, and disasters. Governmental relief capacities also need to be improved. The emergency relief staff of the Agency for International Development (AID) is good, but too small. In expanding it, the foreign aid officials might learn some useful lessons from the Federal Emergency Management Agency.

• *Delineate and divide more clearly the roles of govern-*

ment and nominally private voluntary organizations (PVOs). In some ways, there is little "private" about PVOs, for they typically receive a great part of their funds from the U.S. government; some PVOs, in fact, depend on Washington for as much as 80 percent of their funding. This dependence very often reduces the effectiveness of PVO efforts.

As a general rule, however, PVOs have more flexibility than official U.S. relief efforts. They can also be considerably more cost effective. Nevertheless, there are some emergency functions and services that the U.S. government can undertake more credibly than nongovernmental groups. Finding the proper balance of "private" and government action on a life-saving mission should be determined empirically, based on "comparative advantage." As a general rule, the government should avoid policies that displace voluntary charitable donations, since this would only undercut the basic humanitarian impulse upon which U.S. policies ultimately rest.

• *Improve the early warning systems that may alert countries to approaching famines and disasters.* Aerial surveillance information of the sort collected by the U.S. Department of Agriculture for its global crop assessment and the Commerce Department's meteorological capabilities could help in this regard. Better communication between private groups and government organizations and reduction of barriers created against the international news media in different locations could also greatly strengthen the world's "ground-based" early warning systems.

• *Pre-position emergency relief stocks and trim bureaucratic red tape, particularly requisitioning and payment procedures.* This will cut substantially the lead times in attending to emergencies. The Reagan administration Food for Peace reforms announced in July 1984 were an appropriate step in this direction.

An increased American presence in the field of famine and emergency relief raises an important question and creates an important problem.

The question concerns the appropriate role for international organizations and institutions—particularly such groups as the International Committee of the Red Cross and the UN High Commissioner for Refugees. These groups, under some conditions, have proven highly effective in saving lives during emergencies. It is important to note that such institutions continue to carry credentials of impartiality and internationalism (despite critics' charges that they have not always lived up to these ideals). If it is in the interest of the United States and stricken peoples that relief efforts be international and politically impartial, Washington should encourage international coordination and cooperation in relief activities. At the same time, the United States should expect that such relief efforts not be politically exploited or financially mismanaged.

If the United States makes it clear that it is prepared to cooperate with others, but that it could "go it alone" if political or other difficulties prevent international institutions from contributing effectively to relief efforts, it would demonstrate both a recognition of the possibilities of internationalism and its own commitment to endangered populations. Whatever the United States does, it must ensure that the aid it provides actually reaches those in need and is not diverted or squandered. In some emergencies, therefore, the United States may find it appropriate to use its military resources to transport aid to crisis areas and to distribute the aid to those in need.

The problem concerns the risk of "moral hazard"—the danger that expanded American famine and emergency relief commitments may lead governments in less-developed regions to ignore the distress of their populations or to create outright famine conditions. Moral hazard can never be eliminated completely from any humanitarian commitment, but it can be minimized. One way to do so is to ensure that "emergency relief" is temporary. The history of the UN Relief and Rehabilitation Administration forty years ago gives some insights into how such strictures may be made effective.

A second method to reduce this side effect of aid is through international moral pressure. This is, of course, not always an effective means to force governments to conduct themselves decently; its potential, however, should not be discounted. Publicizing in various forums state acts that cause needless deaths and distress can shame even the most seemingly hardened government, for "killer states" often appreciate the tenuousness of their own claim to legitimate power. Such information may also affect a country's prospects of obtaining additional international aid. Free and unimpeded news reportage is essential for this process. International organizations may also play an important role as impartial observers in conferring opprobrium on offending governments. Their role as impartial observers today carries weight and might, through reforms, be made to carry more.

Development Aid

Redirecting American development policies to the task of encouraging self-sustaining economic growth will require major changes in the operation and direction of government agencies currently charged with promoting economic advance in less-developed countries.

Within a liberal international economic order, it is not the volume of concessional foreign aid that sets the ultimate constraint on a less-developed nation's pace of economic transformation and material progress. Instead, the limit will be set, in practice, principally by the recipient government's policies, administrative competence, and willingness to take advantage of the opportunities afforded by international markets in goods, services, and finance.

Apart from their congressional budget presentations and their election-year pronouncements, current American development policy makers seem to pay strangely little attention to the policy environment in less-developed countries or to the resulting climate of economic incentives and disincentives.[2] Judged by actions rather than words, a principal thrust of current development assistance policies would seem to be the encouragement of international transfer payments to raise living standards through social spending. The rationale for such a policy is to build "human capital." As with any other form of capital, however, the rate of return depends on the manner in which it is put to use. To a distressing extent, the social programs today justified under the rubric of human capital do not create human capital; instead, they fund unproductive public consumption in its name. Such transfers do not encourage self-sustaining growth in most recipient countries. To the contrary, they tend to distort growth processes and economic structures. Moreover, concessional budgetary transfers have often had the effect of overvaluing exchange rates and thereby reducing recipient nations' abilities to compete in, and learn from, the world economy. The consequences of such distortions on the sustainability of emergent structures and the prospects for the poor within them are predictable.

As currently directed, AID conducts a foreign policy that often varies substantially from that of the State Department. This can be seen in AID rules that systematically circumvent the intentions of U.S. human rights legislation, "policy determinations" that undercut State Department positions toward the UN-promoted New International Economic Order or initiatives that either displace private economic activity or tie aid to the purchase of specific American products in a variant of mercantilism. This discrepancy reflects an apparent belief, often embodied in AID documents and official statements, that the international economic order that the United States officially supports cannot work for the poor—or should not be allowed to do so.

American developmental aid should support the workings of just this liberal international economic order. Assistance should be directed toward helping governments govern more productively, rather than redressing international poverty through unsustainable transnational budget transfers. Development assistance should be guided by principles of entrepreneurship and comparative advantage: that is, of making the most productive use of scarce resources through key interventions. The experience of such nonprofit groups as the Rockefeller Foundation and the Ford Foundation in the early post–World War II period demonstrates how tremendously important such a strategic use of charitable money can be for the purposes of promoting material advance.

For the realignment of American development efforts with the purposes of strengthening the liberal order and encouraging improved governance in developing countries, it will be necessary to return to providing technical assistance. Technical assistance was the guiding premise behind U.S. development policies in the early postwar period—the era when many aid recipients "graduated" out of aid and into broad-based self-sustaining economic growth.

To restore U.S. development policies to the tasks of productive technical assistance, many current aid programs must be altered or eliminated. Determining which projects and policies encourage self-sustaining economic growth and increasing government competence is an empirical, not an ideological, question and should be answered through a careful evaluation and review of existing programs. It is likely that new programs will also have to be developed to meet needs in the less-developed countries. In some fields, the requisite know-how for such programs may not yet exist and may have to be created through research and development.

A comprehensive program for development assistance reform cannot be outlined briefly. But components of a reform strategy include:

• *Remove institutional and legislative shackles impairing effectiveness of U.S. development policies.* Organizationally, the present International Development Cooperation Agency (IDCA) separates AID from direct accountability to the State Department. The purposes of AID or any successor organization should be identical with the purposes of overall American foreign policy; for this reason, AID should be brought back fully into the State Department structure. "Congres-

sional notification," restrictions on obligational car-
ryovers, and other special legislative stipulations that
reduce the ability of development officers to design
and administer programs efficiently should be re-
viewed and, where necessary, rescinded.

• *Review U.S. contributions to UN development activities.* To a distressing degree, the programs funded
by the United Nations and related organizations in
the name of "development" are hostile to a free and
open international economy. The United States
should take no part in undermining the system it
helped create, which has promoted prosperity in a
host of once-impoverished lands. Washington should
undertake a thorough review of its UN funding and
stop subsidizing those programs that are found to be
inconsistent with the goals of economic freedom.
Washington should be neither defensive nor apolo-
getic about disinheriting such activities; to the contrary, it should explain clearly the rationale behind
each decision.

• *Cut back "soft" development lending.* There is little
evidence that "soft loans" have special merit in promoting development. To the contrary, very often they
confuse charity and commerce in the view of recipient governments. (This confusion may be relevant to
the current "debt crisis"—a problem whose underlying causes can be traced in part to a tendency to use
commercial loans in less than businesslike ways.)
Transfers of capital to less-developed countries
should be understood as being either charitable or
commercial—not in between. The International Development Authority (IDA) of the World Bank is the
major international vehicle for concessional lending

to less-developed countries. But the projects it finances, if economically sound, should be just as workable under ordinary World Bank auspices. The United States should not replenish IDA funds. It should take a similar position toward the other "soft" lending programs in which it currently participates.

• *Return the World Bank and other multilateral development banks to their original purpose.* As originally envisioned, the International Bank for Reconstruction and Development (IBRD), commonly known as the World Bank, was to serve as a main pillar of a free international economy. It was to promote technical assistance and to encourage the creation of a positive "investment climate" in which economic progress might be hastened. The bank was specifically expected to refrain from displacing private capital or from contributing to national policies that would restrict economic activity in borrowing countries. The bank's present activities, however, do not always seem consistent with these original purposes. The World Bank and other development banks need careful examination, evaluation, and review. Like America's own development institutions, they may usefully be reminded of the purposes for which they were established.

• *Reform P.L. 480.* The U.S. Food for Peace program does not serve developmental goals. In large part, the program's concessional sales strategy is a commodity-disposal project subsidizing U.S. farmers. Unloading cheap American food on the markets of less-developed countries has typically destablized local agriculture and reduced incomes within the rural sector, usually the poorest sector in poor nations.

Only a small portion of current Food for Peace allocations go to emergency or famine relief. A reformed Food for Peace program would increase the volume of food aid earmarked for victims of famines and disasters and diminish allocations for all other purposes.

• *Encourage statistical competence in developing nations.* Governments in the less-developed regions cannot pursue informed social or economic policies unless they have accurate information on social and economic conditions in their countries. This requires domestic statistical systems that can both assess social and economic conditions accurately and monitor changes rapidly and effectively. Many governments lack even the fundamentals of such an apparatus; some, for example, have no solid estimate of such basic factors as their national populations. Demographic, economic, and statistical training to strengthen the data-collecting infrastructure upon which informed governance depends should be a priority form of technical assistance. To the extent that knowledge helps create moral responsibility, better information on national social and economic conditions may also serve as a force for moderation with certain states.

• *Increase technical assistance through U.S. universities.* In such fields as agricultural research, engineering, and health sciences, American universities offer unparalleled opportunities for training. Many other areas of study and research also offer opportunity for strategic transfer of skills and knowledge to selected students from developing countries. A reformed American development program should consider

147

ways in which the resources of America's universities might be put to greater development use, as well as what new capacities might usefully be developed.

• *Expand competitive funding in support of technical innovations for developing countries.* AID's innovative Scientific Research Project and its Strengthening Scientific and Technological Capacity Projects demonstrate how U.S. government funds can encourage research and strengthen technical capacities in developing countries. A similar program may be able to encourage development of devices and technologies of social benefit to developing societies.

• *Develop movable "policy hospitals."* To loosen the constraints of injurious or inefficient indigenous economic policies on the development process, various development specialists could educate rulers and decision makers in developing countries about the economic consequences of policies they have chosen and the alternatives implicit in a variety of strategies that they might pursue instead. This could help foster a lasting competence in dealing with such issues as taxation, finance, budgeting, foreign exchange management, and pricing policies. "Policy hospitals," comprising informed and well-trained personnel, could be sent to receptive states. At present, AID probably lacks the qualified personnel needed for this. Resources for such a program could be drawn from the American academic and business communities; some of the know-how necessary to make such a program operational may have to be developed.

• *Help governments in developing countries make markets work.* The "miracle of the marketplace" is a delicate and complex phenomenon and should not be taken for granted. Markets are not perfectly efficient arbiters of economic activity—if they were, there could not be such a thing as entrepreneurship. A major task confronting a less-developed country is to create the marketing infrastructure that can rapidly and cheaply convey goods and services and information and knowledge. Developing countries must also learn about and understand international markets—including financial ones—if they are to take advantage of the opportunities provided by the international system.

Making markets work, to a great extent, is simply a matter of refraining from predictably destructive interference in their operations. But societies and governments can also take positive actions to create the atmosphere and to build the links and networks upon which efficient and productive markets depend. The United States has much to offer developing countries that wish to improve the functionings of their economies. For example, U.S. business schools train students in the practical aspects of market development; these institutions could teach students and policy makers from less-developed countries as well. Making markets work also depends on the extent to which developing societies successfully build sophisticated and competent financial infrastructures. Training teams such as those developed by the Harvard Institute for International Development may be able to assist here, but in the realm of technical assistance this field remains largely *terra incognita*.

Above all, however, developing countries have much to learn about two fundamentals upon which the effective working of markets is predicated: respect for private property and rule of law. It would be

149

reassuring to think that the United States could contribute to the instruction of low-income countries in this vital area.

• *Encourage U.S. allies to reform their development policies.* A renewed commitment to the principles of the liberal international economic order and to the goal of self-sustaining economic progress will be more effective if emphasized by other Western nations. U.S. allies should consider what their chances of recovering or developing would have been after World War II if the United States had treated them to the same "development" policies they themselves apply to the South today. A dialogue on development reform with other donor nations could greatly increase prospects for the success of both national and cooperative multilateral assistance efforts.

As a final note on development, it should be emphasized, lest there be doubt, that support for a free international economy and commitment to improving policy competence and administrative capacities in less-developed countries are not necessarily code words for enforcing "laissez-faire" internationally. The Republic of China (Taiwan) and South Korea, for example, have performed exceptionally well within a free economy; yet neither is a "minimalist" government. Taipei directs the ROC economy through Four Year Plans and manages a large public enterprise sector that has accounted for as much as two-fifths of the nation's capital formation in certain periods. In Korea, the entire banking and credit system was government run until quite recently; even today the collaboration between government and the "jaebol," or industrial conglomerates, is reminiscent of the situation in Japan in the 1930s. Nevertheless, both countries have been able to take advantage of opportunities from an international economic system that emphasizes results rather than intermediary structures and is thus tolerant of social and political diversity.

The pool of understanding on the many ways in which governments may stimulate economic development is neither as wide nor as deep as might be wished; after more than a generation of international development efforts it sometimes seems as if surprisingly little is known. For this reason, the promotion of competent governance in developing countries should be treated as an empirical, not ideological, issue.

Security Assistance

The purpose of U.S. military and security aid is to apply American power internationally by: first, strengthening the defensive capabilities of states in the American alliance structure; second, helping friendly nations quell internal political or military disturbances; and third, assisting friendly nations in buying breathing space and, with luck, in regaining or retaining stability. On occasion security assistance may be used to buy friendship from governments where this is a commodity for sale.

The premise underlying security assistance is that the extension of U.S. power in the world and the purposes it serves are legitimate. More than any great power, possibly more than any other nation, the American public judges its international initiatives not on the basis of narrow national gains, but by the broader and more demanding standards of moral purpose. If these goals are clear and accepted, as they were in World War II, public support is open ended and wholehearted; if moral purposes appear to be in doubt (as was thought to be the case in the era of Vietnam and Watergate), the use of American power abroad will cost the government and the nation greatly.

The ultimate constraints on security assistance, then, rest on the American people's attitude toward their government and their nation. This attitude is conditioned by trust, which depends in no small degree on the clarity and honesty with which America's leaders explain the international situation and argue for the actions they believe necessary to meet international challenges. Trust is also conditioned by the faithfulness that the nation's leaders show, in words and actions, toward traditional American principles.

Security assistance cannot lead the United States to a foreign policy consensus, but it can play a role in developing domestic support for overseas initiatives. As such, U.S. policy makers must explain honestly what military aid is and what it does. It is not a humanitarian program in any immediate sense. To be sure, the global order that the United States supports is expected, in the long term, to promote humanitarian goals. But money for soldiers and police in a developing nation should not be confused with emergency relief for the victims of disaster.

Just as security assistance is not a humanitarian program, neither is it a development program. Security assistance programs themselves are not meant to spark self-sustaining economic growth in less-developed nations. In fact, the overwhelming emphasis of U.S. security assistance efforts, it may be argued, is on developed nations—through the defense commitment to Japan and NATO. It is simply an accident of geographic and historical circumstances that some of the countries to which Washington extends military and security aid, such as Pakistan and the Sudan, currently happen to have low per capita output.

It is far from certain, moreover, that long-term transfers of money for security purposes promote self-sustaining economic growth. One need only look at current economic events in Egypt and Israel—the two principal recipients of U.S. security assistance funds since the conclusion of the Camp David Accord—to appreciate this. Although security assistance and economic support funds increase a government's freedom to maneuver, what it does with this freedom depends on attitudes and capabilities. (Very different results should be expected in, say, contemporary Singapore and Zaire.) Security assistance is but an instrument to increase a regime's odds of political survival. Political survival is the first concern of governments and rightly so; neither development nor any other positive aim of government can be pursued effectively under a government whose future is in doubt.

Security assistance must be considered separately from humanitarian and development assistance, not only because its purposes are different but also because different rules govern its effective application. Both humanitarian and development aid may have positive effects even when their totals are, in some sense, insufficient. Half the money necessary to prevent all famine deaths, for example, will ameliorate some suffering nonetheless; a quarter of a complete technical assistance program will likely be better than no program at all. This is not the case with military or security assistance. A commitment of only 95 percent of the resources necessary to win a war or stabilize a

regime amounts, in effect, to no commitment at all.
The discontinuous nature of political outcomes and
the uncertainties inherent in them mean that a successful security program will typically err on the side
of excess. Thus, by any economic measure, it will be
open to charges of inefficiency and waste. These
problems cannot be eliminated in a program of political aid but can only be reduced through careful
management.

The effectiveness of security assistance can be
improved through a number of reforms. Among
these:

• *Remove the Economic Support Fund (ESF) from
AID.* Although some of the funds allocated through
the ESF program do go to development projects, this
is essentially coincidental. The purpose of ESF is not
to foster self-sustaining economic development in recipient nations. It is to buy political stability through
financial transfers either by increasing local living
standards directly or by resolving pressing balance-
of-payments difficulties. These objectives are better
described as security related than development ori-
ented. As such, ESF should be administered with
programs having similar goals.

• *Reduce the soft lending component and raise the
direct grant portion within the mixture of American security
assistance funds.* Concessional lending for development has blurred the line between charity and commerce; by the same token, as Jeffrey Bergner has
argued,[3] soft lending for security assistance has seriously confused donors and recipients over the distinctions between commercial transactions and strategic commitments. Security lending, moreover, has

had unexpected adverse economic consequences on borrowers. Making clear distinction between military-security grants and military sales would force American policy makers to define their objectives more clearly. The United States may also wish to consider "loan forgiveness" for some or all of its security assistance debtor accounts.

• *Reform the legislation governing security assistance.* Since 1974, when it was reported that Uruguayan police receiving U.S. security aid were torturing political prisoners, the Congress has prohibited the United States from providing security training or assistance to nonmilitary organizations in recipient countries. The practical consequences of this have been perverse. In El Salvador, for example, it is widely believed that right-wing "death squads" operated from within the sanctum of the national police agencies; of all organs of government in El Salvador, these were the only ones to which the United States could not apply money and therefore had least leverage with which to demand reforms.

These unintended effects are not unique to El Salvador. Many countries in Latin America have small standing armies; Costa Rica and several Caribbean states have no army at all. In such nations national security and law enforcement duties both fall under the aegis of the police force, but current laws prevent the United States from aiding such societies through security programs. In recent years, one Caribbean country was convulsed by an uprising of Rastafarian revolutionaries intent on seizing the government; another experienced a coup attempt by Ku Klux Klan–inspired forces. In neither case could Washington provide necessary security help, for neither had a standing army. Under current U.S. laws, receiving American military or security assistance would require friendly societies in the hemisphere to militarize, thus altering their peaceable civilian traditions or to request the outright stationing of U.S. troops.[4]

Surely U.S. laws can do better than this. Restricting the ability of the U.S. government to conduct foreign policy is no real substitute for embuing official policies with the moral purposes Americans expect in them.

Conclusion

Foreign aid policies should be used to reinforce U.S. political, economic, and moral objectives throughout the world because these objectives are fundamentally sound. The converse to this argument and its implications is important as well. If America's fundamental political, economic, and moral purposes in the world are sound, then strengthening U.S. power is in itself a beneficial and effective form of foreign aid.

Building American might is in part a military task, but only in part. America's economic strength and its economic contribution to a free international economy will depend critically on the extent to which the nation remains true to its professed principles of free trade. The U.S. government's success in bringing spending in line with revenues will affect the prospects for the economic security not only of Americans but also of people all over the world. And America's performance in maintaining the dollar as a stable and reliable currency will have a continuing impact on the prospects for world commerce and international economic growth. Finally, the honesty and decency with

156

which the United States conducts its international policies will have far-reaching consequences, for the United States is not just a nation: it is an idea.

More than three decades ago, Eric Johnston, the Point Four (third world foreign aid) adviser to Presidents Truman and Eisenhower, reflected on America's role in the world:

> We are living in the last half of the twentieth century, and the scepter of world leadership has been thrust in our hands. I don't think most of us wanted it, but we have it just the same. We find ourselves in competition for the minds of men with imperialistic, expansionistic communism. That competition, in my opinion, will run for a long period of time. . . . I am one of those who believe the human wants of mankind are insatiable. The problem is how to provide an opportunity to meet them. . . . I believe that the foreign policy of America, though not clearly enunciated—and I wish we would clearly enunciate it . . . is to export the good things of the 20th century to other peoples. It would be a terrible mistake for us to export but a portion of those things. . . .[5]

Little basic progress has been made in resolving the underlying problems to which Johnston referred. Yet his words remain the words of enormous hope. What Johnston realized then and what Americans should know today is that no other nation has ever been in as good a position as the United States to champion the cause of the world's poor. Americans should recognize the responsibilities this implies, but they may also rejoice at the extraordinary coincidence of interests between a strong and healthy America and the prospects of advancement for the impoverished and unprotected peoples of the earth.

Notes

1. George F. Kennan, "Our Aid to Russia: A Forgotten Chapter," *New York Times Magazine,* July 19, 1959; quoted in Benjamin M. Weissman, *Herbert Hoover and Famine Relief to Soviet Russia, 1921–1923* (Stanford, Calif.: Hoover Institution Press, 1974), p. xi.

2. The story of AID's performance during President Reagan's first term of office cannot be fully developed in this short, prescriptive chapter. Suffice it to say that elements of the story include the steady subordination of policy questions to public relations concerns, a reluctance or indifference to the restoration of policy competence within the agency, and a drift in a direction that contradicted many of the bipartisan objectives the president himself had laid down. A fuller expansion on this topic may be found in chapter 1, "The Perversion of Foreign Aid."

3. Jeffrey T. Bergner, "Security Assistance," in Doug Bandow, ed., *U.S. Aid to the Developing World: A Free Market Agenda* (Washington, D.C.: Heritage Foundation, 1985).

4. I am indebted to Bruce McColm of Freedom House for this information.

5. Eric Johnston, Testimony before the Subcommittee on Foreign Economic Policy of the House Committee on Foreign Affairs, April 30, 1953; reprinted in U.S. Congress, *Foreign Economic Policy* (Washington, D.C.: 1953), p. 309.

Index

postwar outlays, 4–6, 7, 31, 78–80
purpose and rationale, 1–5, 25–28, 69–70, 135–36
recipients' perspectives, 26–28, 87
Soviet aid to Cuba, 125–26
subordination to military objectives, 31–36
See also Military assistance
Foreign Assistance Act of 1967, 39
Foreign Assistance Act of 1973, 37–39
Foreign policy, 44–47, 144. *See also* Liberal international order
France, 4

Germany, 11, 23, 83
Germany, West, 25
Ghana, 99, 104, 106–7
Global 2000 report, 48–51
Greece, 4, 32, 39, 84
Guinea, 98

Hanoi, 40
Health assistance, 53
Helms, Jesse, 59–60
Himmelfarb, Gertrude, 8
Hoffer, Eric, 13
Holland, 84
Hoover, Herbert, 3, 137
Hopper, W. David, 114
"Human capital" argument, 86, 93–100, 142
Humanitarian aid. *See* Natural disasters
Humphrey, Hubert, 28–29
Hurricanes, 71

India, 39, 82, 84, 105
Indonesia, 75
Industrial policies, 26–27, 83–84

Infant mortality, 23, 55, 56, 128
International Bank for Reconstruction and Development. *See* World Bank
International Development Association (IDA), 31, 145–46
International Development Cooperation Agency (IDCA), 47, 144
International Labor Organization, 44
International Monetary Fund (IMF), 21, 45–46, 89, 116
Investment
climate, 22, 26
direct private, 81
mismanagement, 73, 85, 97, 108, 125, 143, 145
Iran, 32
Israel, 153
Italy, 84
Ivory Coast, 107

Jamaica, 84
Japan, 71, 84, 85, 107–8, 127
Johnson, Harry, xi
Johnston, Eric, 33, 157
Jordan, 11

Kennan, George, 137
Kennedy administration, 33–34
Kenya, 96, 98–99
Kissinger, Henry, 45–46

Land reform, 59–62
Latin American debt crisis
assessment of creditor nations' policies, 121–26
capital mismanagement, 129–31
effect on democratization, 11–12, 122, 131–32
effect on life expectancy, 121–22, 126–28

INDEX

West Pakistan. *See* Pakistan
World Bank
  establishment and objectives,
    5–6, 21–22, 89, 145–46
  population assistance, 95–96
  programs and policies, 41–
    43, 114–15

soft loans, 30–31, 145
structural adjustment loans,
  112, 115
World War II, 3, 22–25

Zaire, 87, 97

About the Author

NICHOLAS EBERSTADT is a visiting scholar at the American Enterprise Institute for Public Policy Research and a visiting fellow at the Harvard University Center for Population Studies. He has served as a consultant to the U.S. Agency for International Development, the World Bank, and the U.S. Department of State on various aspects of policy pertaining to economic development in low-income countries and has published more than seventy articles and papers on questions of policy and development in Communist and non-Communist areas. Mr. Eberstadt is the editor of *Fertility Decline in the Less Developed Countries* and author of *Poverty in China* and *The Poverty of Communism*. Mr. Eberstadt holds degrees from Harvard College, the London School of Economics, and the Kennedy School of Government.

*This book was edited by Dana Lane
of the publications staff
of the American Enterprise Institute.
The index was prepared by Patricia Ruggiero.
The text was set in Baskerville.
Coghill Book Typesetting Company, of Richmond, Virginia,
set the type, and Edwards Brothers Incorporated,
of Ann Arbor, Michigan, printed and bound the book,
using permanent, acid-free paper.*